Financial Strategies and Topics in Finance

Selected Public Lectures of
Professor Harold Bierman, Jr.
from 1960–2015

Financial Strategies and Topics in Finance

Selected Public Lectures of Professor Harold Bierman, Jr. from 1960–2015

Harold Bierman, Jr

Cornell University

W JERSEY • LONDON • SINGAPORE • BEIJING • SHANGHAI • HONG KONG • TAIPEI • CHENNAI • TOKYO

Published by

World Scientific Publishing Co. Pte. Ltd.

5 Toh Tuck Link, Singapore 596224

USA office: 27 Warren Street, Suite 401-402, Hackensack, NJ 07601

UK office: 57 Shelton Street, Covent Garden, London WC2H 9HE

Library of Congress Cataloging-in-Publication Data
Names: Bierman, Harold, author.
Title: Financial strategies and topics in finance: selected public lectures of professor
Harold Bierman, Jr. from 1960–2015 / Harold Bierman, Jr (Cornell University).
Description: 1 Edition. | New Jersey : World Scientific, [2018] | Includes bibliographical references.
Identifiers: LCCN 2017045437| ISBN 9789813222885 | ISBN 9789813222892 (pbk)
Subjects: LCSH: Finance. | Investments.
Classification: LCC HG173 .B494 2018 | DDC 332--dc23
LC record available at https://lccn.loc.gov/2017045437

British Library Cataloguing-in-Publication Data
A catalogue record for this book is available from the British Library.

For any available supplementary material, please visit
http://www.worldscientific.com/worldscibooks/10.1142/10515#t=suppl

Desk Editor: Shreya Gopi

Typeset by Stallion Press
Email: enquiries@stallionpress.com

Printed in Singapore

Contents

Preface

This is a collection of public lectures on the subject of corporate finance given around the world during the period 1960–2015. Among the places visited are:

Shanghai, China
Tokyo, Japan
Seoul, Korea
Paris, France
London, England
Leuven, Belgium
Brussels, Belgium
Rotterdam, Holland
New York and Ithaca, New York.

This book does not include classroom lectures but rather public lectures to mixed audiences. Hopefully, they communicate the flavor of an academic viewpoint of actual corporate finance.

Hal Bierman
November 2017

List of Acronyms

401K	A type of investment account
AT&T	American Telephone and Telegraph Corporation
CEO	Chief executive officer
CFROGI	Cash flow, return on gross investment
CS	Common stock
DCF	Discounted cash flow
DJIA	Dow Jones Industrial Average
DRIP	Dividend reinvestment plan
ECC	Economic cost of capital
EPS	Earnings per share
FIFO	'First in, first out' flow of inventory
IRA	Investment retirement account
IRR	Internal rate of return
LBO	Leveraged buyout
LIFO	'Last in, first out' flow of inventory
M+A	Mergers and acquisitions (investment banking activity)
MBO	Management buyout
NCR	National Cash Register (a manufacturer and seller of business machines)
NPV	Net present value
NYSE	New York Stock Exchange
PERCS	Preferred earnings common stock
PS	Preferred stock
ROA	Return on assets
ROE	Return on equity
ROI	Return on investment
S+L	Savings and loan (a form of bank)
SRA	Supplementary retirement account
WACC	Weighted average cost of capital

About the Author

Harold Bierman, Jr is the Nicholas H Noyes Professor Emeritus of Business Administration at Cornell University, USA. He was at Cornell for 59 years, before which, he taught at the University of Chicago and the University of Michigan. Before his Ph.D., he taught at Louisiana State University (Baton Rouge, LA).

He has been a consultant for many public organizations and industrial firms and is the author of more than 200 books and articles in the fields of accounting, finance, investment, taxation and quantitative analysis. In 1985, he was named the winner of the prestigious Dow Jones Award of the American Assembly of Collegiate Schools of Business for his outstanding contributions to collegiate management education.

Lecture 1

Ten Money Makers

No date and no audience identified.

List of Ten Financial Money Makers for a Corporation

1. Pension payment timing is important.
2. LIFO is desirable (if you are using FIFO fire CEO and outside directors).
3. Debt > PS, CS > PS. Why do firms use PS?
4. Retained earnings versus Dividends and new capital. Which costs less?
5. Stock acquisition[1] versus dividends.
6. Buy versus lease.
7. Should one borrow long or short term? How much?
8. Bond refunding decisions. Can you make money if interest rates go up?
9. Do not use payback[2] or ROI (time value and long-term analysis).
10. Do not use IRR for mutually exclusive investments.

[1]Stock acquisition: Stock repurchase by issuing corporation.
[2]Payback: Time required to earn an amount equal to investment.

Lecture 2

Ten Financial Positions

The date and purpose of this presentation are not known, but it seems like a sensible message.

Ten Financial Positions

1. Cannot forecast interest rates (we can determine the market's forecasts).
2. Cannot forecast future stock prices (markets are relatively efficient) or know market turns (we can think the market is becoming too high or too low).
3. Common dollar accounting or other types of price level accounting are difficult to use effectively to measure performance and are not normally useful to make decisions.
4. "No risk" investments do not require risk adjustments. Some acceptable investments may earn less than the WACC.
5. Some investments expecting to earn more than the WACC are not acceptable.
6. Debt versus common stock is skewed in favor of debt.
7. "Buy low, sell high" is bad advice.
8. A decision that causes the EPS of the next period to decrease may be a desirable decision.
9. A banker and a financial officer of a manufacturing firm may agree on the facts and properly disagree on the decision to offer credit to a specific customer.
10. Look for tax arbitrage situations.

Lecture 3

Famous Strategies

No date and no identification as to purpose of talk.

Famous Strategies

1. Navy: Cross the T.
2. Army: Get there "firstest" with "moistest".
3. Leo[1]: Good guys finish last (therefore be "bad").
4. Hayes[2]: Three yards and a cloud of dust. Do not pass. Two out of three outcomes are bad.
5. McGuire[3]: Two technicals motivate the team twice as much as one T.
6. IBM: Think.
7. Boy Scouts: Be prepared.

[1] Leo Durocher: Manager of the Brooklyn Dodgers and then of the New York Giants in the 1930s.

[2] Ohio State football coach Woody Hayes.

[3] Al McGuire, a famous college basketball coach.

Lecture 4

The Sustainable Growth Rate

The Sustainable Growth Rate: No Debt

$$\begin{aligned} E_1 &= E + (rb)E \\ &= E(1 + rb) = E(1 + g). \end{aligned}$$

Therefore, $g = rb$, with no debt.
Symbols:

r	is the return on new investments.
b	is the retention rate.
E	is the earnings of the initial year.

Sustainable Growth Rate: With Debt

	New Earnings from Retention	New Earnings from New Dept	After Tax Interest Cost on $\frac{B}{S}(bE)$ of dept
$E(1+g) = E$	$+rbE$	$+\left[r\frac{B}{S}(bE) -\right.$	$\left.(1-t)k_i\frac{B}{S}(bE)\right]$

$$g = rb + \frac{B}{S}b[r - (1 - t)k_i].$$

Example (Using Debt)

Let $\frac{B}{S} = .30$, $r = .15$, $t_c = .35$, $k_i = .10$,

$b = .60, (1 - t_c)k_i = .065$

$$g = rb + b[r - k_i]\frac{B}{S}$$

$$= .15(.60) + .60[.15 - .065].30 = .09 + .053 = .1053.$$

If E = \$10, then \$6 is retained, \$1.80 is borrowed and \$7.80 is invested. The \$7.80 earns .15 or \$1.17, after tax interest of \$1.80 × .065 = .117 is paid and the next increase in earnings is \$1.05. The new earnings are \$11.05 or a .105 increase in earnings.

	Year 1	Year 2	Year 3
Earnings	10.0	11.05	12.21
Retained	6.0	6.63	7.33
Dividends	4.0	4.42	4.88
g	0.105	0.105	0.105
Increment to Earnings	1.105	1.16	

What factors affect growth that are not included in the sustainable growth formula?

1. Unexpected inflation
2. Increased efficiency
3. Utilization of excess capacity (sales growth)
4. Changes in prices of products sold or bought
5. Change in debt cost
6. Change in product mix
7. Game the accounting rules (e.g., cut-back R&D)
8. Expectations of growth model are not realized for one or more variables
9. Mergers and Acquisitions
10. Restructuring
11. New capital (or divestments)

Preferred Stock ($t_c = .35$)

Assume \$100 preferred is paying \$8 per year.

$$k_p = .08 \text{ After tax cost}$$

$$\frac{.08}{1 - .35} = .123 \text{ Before tax cost}$$

Debt

Assume a \$1,000 bond is paying \$80 interest.

$$(1 - t_c)k_i = (1 - .35).08 = .052 \text{ After Tax Cost}$$
$$.08 \text{ Before Tax Cost}$$

Convertible Debt (convertible into 20 shares of common)

Assume a \$1,000 bond pays \$6 interest.

$$(1 - t_c)k = (1 - .35).06 = .039 \text{ After Tax Cost}$$
$$.06 \text{ Before Tax Cost}$$

But these convertible bond costs understate the cost to the corporation which must include the cost of the option to convert.

Straight Debt versus Convertible

Straight debt costs .08

Convertible bond "costs" .06. The bond is convertible into 20 shares.

A one year horizon.

If $P_1 = \$60$, which security is best?

If $P_1 = \$50$, which security is best?

$\mathbf{P_1 = \$60}$

$$\text{Outlay with straight debt} = \$1{,}080$$
$$\text{Outlay with convertible} = \$1{,}200 \text{ or } \$1{,}260.$$

$\mathbf{P_1 = \$50}$

$$\text{Outlay with convertible} = \$1{,}000 \text{ or } \$1{,}060.$$

Lecture 5

What Does a School of Management Teach?

I suspect I never gave this talk, but it is a reasonable talk (and short).

What Does a School of Management Teach? A Partial Inventory

a. Wisdoms
b. Skills and Language (e.g., accounting)
c. Institutions
d. Theories
e. Applications (cases, games)

More Specifically

1. Marginal analysis (versus use of averages) and other basic economic concepts
2. Time discounting
3. Comparative advantage, monopolistic competition and the virtues of free trade
4. Valuing information (sampling)
5. Decision theory (state act consequence)
6. Opportunity costs
7. Economic incentives and markets (self-interest)
8. Optimization (e.g., an inventory model or linear programming). Maximization

9. Portfolio theory (diversification)
10. Real versus illusions (as in capital structure and vertical slices)

But the Important Things to be Learned Are:

1. How to interact and work effectively with others.
2. How to manage and how to organize.
3. How to speak and to write effectively.
4. How to evaluate alternatives (think).
5. A code of morality for management (help solve social problems).

Lecture 6

Economic Income versus Economic Value Added

Introduction

The term "residual income" has been replaced by "economic value added." While the EVA calculation is an excellent calculation, the name "Economic Income" is more accurate. The calculation used in practice does not measure the economic value added.

Economic Income versus Economic Value Added

As early as 1965, David Solomons advocated the use of residual income to measure performance. Residual income is the normal accounting net income minus an interest cost on all capital utilized in earning the income. In 1970 Keith Schwayder wrote:

> Recently, many writers have suggested that residual income be substituted for or supplemented to return on investment analysis.

Now we fast forward to 1993 and the article titled "The Real Key to Creating Wealth" in *Fortune* by Shawn Tully advocating economic value added (EVA). If the term "residual income" is to be replaced, should the replacing term be economic income (EI) or economic value added (EVA)? The income being considered is a measure of the results of operations, not a comprehensive income measure.

We will consider:

a. why EVA is a misleading name if it is applied to the economic income measure.
b. how the economic income measure can be improved.

Economic Value Added

The name "residual income" never attracted any significant attention in the business community. The name economic value added (EVA) is now catching managers' attention. There are two reasons for evaluating the name to be used. First, the name used should be descriptive of the calculation. Secondly, the name of the calculation should better enable us to understand the economic significance of the calculation.

To illustrate the calculations assume the following investment with a four year life and a .20 internal rate of return (the investment has a .10 capital cost).

Time: i	Cash Flows	PV of Benefits (.10) at time i
0	−4,000	4,830.13
1	1,800	3,513.15
2	1,600	2,264.46
3	1,400	1,090.91
4	1.200	
NPV (.10) =	830.13	

The investment's net present value at time zero is $830.13. Assume that straight line depreciation is used. The economic incomes for each year are:

	Year 1	Year 2	Year 3	Year 4
Revenue	1,800	1,600	1,400	1,200
Depreciation	1,000	1,000	1,000	1,000
Interest Cost (.10)	400	300	200	100
Economic Income	400	300	200	100

The present value of the economic incomes is:

$$\text{PV} = \frac{400}{1.1} + \frac{300}{(1.1)^2} + \frac{200}{(1.1)^3} + \frac{100}{(1.1)^4} = \$830.13$$

The present value of the economic incomes is equal to the NPV of the investment using the cash flows. This equality always holds and is independent of the accounting depreciation method being used.

The term "economic income" is consistent with the subtraction of the interest cost on the capital used, and the fact that the present value of the economic incomes is equal to the theoretically correct NPV measure of value (assuming that .10 is the appropriate discount rate).

Now, consider the economic value added (EVA) term and whether or not this title is applicable. Assume that the first year's operations are as expected and the economic income is $400. Is this the economic value added? The investment's value at time zero is $4,830.13. At time one the value is the $3,513.15 value of the asset plus $1,800 of cash generated or in total $5,313.15. This is a value added during the year of $483.01 (or .10 of $4,830.13). The $400 of economic income is not equal to the economic value added. The economic value added is an entirely different concept than the economic income. The $483.02 is a good measure of value added during the year. The $400 of economic income measures the value added by operations, and does not consider the asset's change in present value.

To better understand the $483.01 of economic value added, assume the $4,000 investment cost is written-up to $4,830.13 of value at time zero. The $1,800 of time one cash flow has a time zero cost of $\frac{1,800}{1.10} = \$1,636.36$. For the first year, we now have:

Revenue		$1,800.00
Value Based Depreciation		1,636.36
Net		$ 163.64
Interest Earned on Value:		
4,830.13 × .10 =	$483.01	

Interest Cost on \$1,636.36:		
1,636.36 × .10 =	16364	319.37
Value Added		\$483.01

This concept, while interesting in a theoretical sense, is too abstract to be of use to operating management. The \$483.01 interest earned on value represents the increase in value since all the cash flows are one period closer to being collected. The interest cost is the interest expense associated with the \$1,800 of revenue earned in year one (and the \$1,636.36 asset).

The economic income measure of \$400 is not equal to the \$483.01 measure of the year's value added.

Economic Depreciation

Define economic depreciation to be the difference in the asset's present value at two moments in time. The first year's economic depreciation is $4{,}830.13 - 3{,}513.15 = \$1{,}316.98$ (the asset is recorded at its present value rather than its cost or alternatively you can assume the asset costs \$4,830.13). The value added is \$483.02 or:

Revenue	\$1,800.00
Economic Depreciation	1,316.98
Income or Value Added	\$ 483.02

The income is \$483.00 and is equal to the value added. The economic income is:

Revenue		\$1,800.00
Depreciation	\$1,316.98	
Interest	483.02	1,800.00
Economic Income		\$ 0

Using economic depreciation the economic income is \$0 while the value added is \$483.02. Obviously they are not equivalent measures or concepts.

To consider another variation of the situation assume the discount rate (interest rate) for the investment is .20 rather than .10.

Now when \$1,800 of revenue is earned in year 1, the economic depreciation is \$1,000 and the economic income is equal to zero (the interest cost is now \$800). But the asset's initial value is \$4,000 and the value at the year's end is \$3,000 plus the \$1,800 of cash. The economic value added is \$800 even though the economic income is zero. The results of operations were equal to zero (assuming the \$1,000 of depreciation and \$800 of interest are correct), but the other changes that took place result in the economic value added to be \$800. The computation of the value added would be:

Revenue	\$1,800	
Value Based Depreciation	1,500	$\left(\text{equal to } \frac{1,800}{1.2} = \$1,500\right)$
Net	300	
Interest Earned on Value		
4,000 × .20 = \$800		
Interest Cost		
1,500 × .20 = 300	300	
Value Added	\$ 800	

Note that the value based depreciation is not equivalent to economic (present value) depreciation which includes elements of interest (the asset's value changes).

The economic income is computed taking into consideration the opportunity cost of the capital that is used during the period. Thus with a .20 interest rate the economic income of the first year is zero. The economic value added should measure the change in value between two moments in time. As illustrated above the two concepts are different.

But what if the term economic value added is more persuasive in the marketplace than economic income? If a term is to be used over the long term, then the term should be consistent with an intuitive interpretation of what it means. The income measure that is commonly called EVA is not equivalent to the economic value added by the investment and the term should not be applied to that income measure. Economic income is a much more appropriate term.

Lecture 7

Distribution Policy

Alternatives

1. Retained earnings
2. Cash dividends
3. Share repurchase
4. DRIP (Dividend Reinvestment Plan)
5. Stock dividends
6. Sale of business (combined with retained earnings)

Reasons for Dividends

1. Zero Tax Investors or Different Tax Laws
2. Expectations of Investors: A Signal to Investors
3. "Trust Legal List"
4. No Good Investments: A Low Opportunity Cost
5. Large g attracts analysts
6. Do Right by Investors: (Conscience and Ethics)
7. Others Do It (Stock price effect)
8. Reduce Risk (Bird in Hand)
9. Transaction Costs of Investors Who Want Cash

Share repurchase is very light to difficult competition to beat.

Lecture 8

Stock Price is Too High

What should the CEO do?

1. Sell the stock he/she owns.
2. Acquire other corporations using the overvalued stock.
3. Do not inflate stock prices further. Be careful when discussing financials.
4. Use convertible debt (low cost).
5. Investigate whether substituting debt for equity can adequately increase stock value.
6. Investigate whether eliminating cash dividend can increase stock value.

Lecture 9

Drivers of Common Stock Prices

Given somewhere in Europe between 1985–1995.

The Market Evaluates Stock Price Using:

a. Current earnings
   Current earnings before interest and taxes (EBIT)
   Current free cash flow (EBITDA)
   Current change in stock equity
b. Forecasted earnings and revenues
   Forecasted EBIT
   Forecasted free cash flow (EBITDA)
c. The forecasted earnings are affected by the expected growth rate of earnings.
d. The discount rate (time value factor) affects the present value of the forecasts.
e. Combining (b) and (c) and (d), the price is determined by the present value of all future cash distributions made by the firm (dividends broadly defined). The form of the distribution is important (investor taxes).
f. The stock's risk affects the discount rate, see (d).
g. General economic climate and health of the capital and stock markets.

Cost of Common Stock

The discounted cash flow mode

If dividends grow forever at a rate g and if $k_e > g$, then:

$$P_0 = \frac{D_1}{k_e - g}.$$

Solving for k_e

$$k_e = \frac{D_1}{P_0} + g.$$

This relationship is widely used to estimate the cost of equity capital.

Remember, it is necessary that $k_e > g$ for the above two formulations to apply.

Complexities:

It is difficult to estimate g.
Dividends may now be equal to zero.
g might change through time.

Example:

Let $D_1 = \$10$, $k_e = .12$, $g = .11$

$$P_0 = \frac{D_1}{k_e - g} = \frac{10}{.12 - .11} = \$1{,}000$$

If k_e increases to .13, then a dramatic decrease in P_0:

$$P_0 = \frac{10}{.13 - .11} = \$500.$$

If $k_e = .12$ and $g = .02$, then:

$$P_0 = \frac{10}{.12 - .02} = \$100.$$

If $g = .13$, then:

$$P_0 = \frac{10}{.12 - (-.13)} = \$40.$$

You can modify assumption of constant growth and can have many different growth rates.

P/E Multiplier

Define $D_1 = (1-b)E$, where b is the retention rate and E is earnings:

$$P_0 = \frac{(1-b)E}{k_e - g}$$

Dividing by E:

$$\frac{P_0}{E} = \frac{1-b}{k_e - g}$$

where $g = rb$. $= \dfrac{1-b}{k_e - g}$ is an estimate of what the P/E should be if b, k, and g are known.

If $r = k_e$

$$P_0 = \frac{(1-b)E}{k_e - k_e b} = \frac{(1-b)E}{(1-b)k_e} = \frac{E}{k_e}$$

and

$$k_e = \frac{E}{P_0}.$$

If $b = 0$, then $g = rb = 0$ and again $k_e = \dfrac{E}{P_0}$.

Determination of cost of equity

1. DCF Model: $k_e = \dfrac{D_1}{P_0} + g$
2. $k_e = \frac{E}{P_0}$ if $r = k_e$ on new investment or $b = 0$.
3. CAPM: $k_e = r_f + (\bar{r}_m - r_f)\beta$
4. Ask stockholders.
5. Add C basis points to yield of Treasuries, Triple A's, firm's debt, or preferred stock. Difficult to justify C.
6. Historical ROE for firm or market (not recommended).

Conclusion: The cost of equity is difficult to determine.

Lecture 10

Costs of Capital: An Overview of Finance

This lecture was given in Louvain, Belgium.

We Want to Consider the Costs of:

a. Common stock
b. Preferred stock
c. Straight debt
d. Convertible debt
e. Retained earnings
f. The weighted average cost of capital

Cost of Debt

Symbols

Let

k_i	be contractual cost of debt
B	be amount of debt
S	be amount of stock
V	be size of firm ($V = S + B$)
I	be contractual interest amount ($I = k_i B$)

Ten risks to investors of buying debt

a. Default of Delay (credit risk) of Payment
b. Interest Rate
c. Inflation
d. Exchange Rate
e. Call Risk
f. Loss of Security (Bearer Bond)
g. Common Stock Does Better (opportunity cost)
h. Bond rating change
i. Thin market for the Security (costly to sell)
j. Event risk

What factors affect cost of debt?

a. Market (Fed & Treasury), Level of r_f. Opportunity cost.
b. Bond rating. Credit risk.
c. Firm's strategy: Use of funds.
d. Leverage (financial) — Liquidity position.
e. Duration (maturity) — Serial, sinking fund.
f. Call — Coupon Size (Bearer-Registered) - Put.
g. Subordination: Asset security.
h. Covenants (safeguards).
i. Conversion & Warrants.
j. Size of firm & Size of issue (liquidity).
k. Age of firm & financial record.
l. Tax status of firm. Tax rules and rates for issuer.
m. Income & Cash Flow — Coverages.
n. Relations with banks — Wall Street.
o. Intangibles (management, products, strategies).
p. Inflation.
q. Exchange Rate (currency).
r. Limited Recourse: Security.
s. Government, Corporate, Personal Guarantee.
t. Event risk protection.
u. Tax rules for investors for debt and other securities.

Interest rate

a. Floating or fixed.
b. Floating but convertible into fixed.
c. Zero coupon.
d. Low coupon.
e. Price level adjustment.
f. Tied to: Income, dividends, Treasuries, NYSE level or volume.
g. Interest payable in stock or in kind.
h. Currency.
i. Contingent, reset, deferrable.
j. Different rates in different years.

Cost of debt

Before tax cost $= k_i$

The debt saves tk_i of taxes, therefore

After Tax Cost $= (1 - t_c)k_i$ where t_c is the corporate tax rate.

If debt and equity both cost k_i and if $L = \frac{B}{V}$, then the WACC (k_0) is:

$$k_0 = (1 - L)k_i + L(1 - t_c)k_i$$

$$k_0 = (1 - t_cL)k_i$$

Example:

A company with a tax rate of .35 uses .40 of debt that costs .10. Equity also costs .10. The after tax cost of funds is:

$k_0 = (1 - .40 \times .35).10 = .086$ (No risk premium for equity.)

Zero dept: $k_0 = .10$.

100% dept : $k_0 = .065$.

With zero debt:

$$k_0 = .10$$

With 100% debt:

$$k_0 = .10 - .35(.10) - .065$$

or equivalently:

$$k_0 = (1 - k_c)k_i = (1 - .35).10 = .065.$$

Of course, the assumption that debt and equity cost the same is not correct.

Return to investor

1. Current "yield".
2. Yield to maturity.
3. Yield to first call.
4. Yield to later call.
5. Return with sinking fund (or multiple of sinking fund).
6. Yield to yield.

Yield to yield

20 years to maturity for $1,000 bond.
.06 level interest Price = $659.45.
Yield to Maturity is .10.

$$\begin{aligned} 1{,}000(1.10)^{-20} &= \$148.64 \\ 60B(20.10) &= \underline{\ \ 510.81} \\ &\ \$659.45 \end{aligned}$$

Lecture 11

Debt Limits for Corporations

No date for this talk but somewhere between 1986 and 2005 would be my guess. Probably given in New York City.

Debt Limits for Corporations

There are many valid reasons for corporations to use debt. The objective of this talk is to define the factors that may or may not limit the amount of debt issued by a firm.

There are two somewhat neglected reasons for not issuing debt. One is that a large part of the burden of bad outcomes falls on management. The second is that for some firms the issuance of debt in substitution of common stock adversely affects earnings per share.

We will initially offer three reasons for a corporation to issue debt. First, if the expected return from the assets to be acquired exceeds the after tax cost of debt, the expected income from incremental debt issuance is positive. Secondly, given the current tax laws, the issuance of debt in substitution for common stock can increase the expected wealth of the common stockholders. Third, the use of debt reduces the amount of stock equity capital that is needed for a given investment plan.

The Extreme Case of No Debt Limit

The economy's experience during 2007–2009 highlighted the extreme case of there being no limit to the amount of debt firms can issue. There are corporations (and managers) who will issue debt as long as the expected return of the assets to be purchased is larger than the after tax cost of debt. The case studies of Lehman Brothers, Merrill Lynch, and Citi Group illustrate the willingness of some financial institutions to remove all limits of the amount of debt they will issue. These cases were all after the collapse of Long Term Capital Management ten years earlier that made it clear that too large an amount of risky assets financed largely by debt can lead to financial disasters.

An inspection of a firm's balance sheet can reveal the percentage of the capital structure that is debt, but this tells us little about the firm's risk until a study of the riskiness of the firm's assets is conducted.

For example, assume 90% of a firm's assets are financial securities. Furthermore, assume that all of the securities are defined to be investment grade by the rating agencies. But, unfortunately, one cannot accept the bond ratings but rather there must be independent analyses and even then one cannot be sure that the credit evaluators have sound judgment. We live in a world with uncertainty.

Thus even with high grade investments, limits should be set by management on the percentage of the capital that is debt. Working against the concept of operational debt limits is the fact that the financial models may show that the expected return of equity will be increased by using debt or by substituting debt for equity.

Thus without strict debt regulation by an oversight agency there is a natural tendency for a profit maximizing management to increase the amount of risky assets offering an expected return larger than the after tax cost of debt and to finance these assets with an ever increasing percentage of debt (to increase the return on equity). A management that insists on using equity to finance the risky assets may likely find itself being beaten in the marketplace for resources by firms using more debt.

Consider Merrill Lynch as of December 31, 2007. Total stockholders' equity was $32 billion. Short-term borrowings and deposits were $470 billion and long-term borrowings were $261 billion or total debt was $731 billion. This debt measure excluded the debt equivalents of derivatives or the debt of non-consolidated subsidiaries. Twenty-three dollars of debt for every dollar of equity is a large amount of debt. Lehman Brothers had even more debt, a large amount of which was not on its year-end balance sheet.

Despite the above temptations, we can find that there are long-lived corporations that resist the siren call of financing too much risky assets with too much debt. The next section will consider the factors that act as controls on the amount of debt.

Factors Limiting the Amount of Debt

The list of factors limiting the amount of debt issued by a corporation in substitution of equity is long. They include:

1. The economic characteristics of the firm's assets limit the amount of debt that can rationally be supported. Also, potential lenders may be reluctant to lend.
2. Management may say no to expansion with debt because of the expected costs of financial distress and bankruptcy. Adding debt increases the incremental risk to shareholders arising from financial distress and increases the variance of outcomes for stockholders.
3. The probability of timely utilization of tax savings from the debt interest is less than one, reducing the incremental expected value from substituting $1 of debt for equity as additional debt is issued.
4. The owners and/or managers fear loss of control because of the risk of bankruptcy. Bankruptcy might prevent the firm and its management from reaching a future pot of gold. Also, debt indenture provisions limit managerial actions. Incremental debt limits the managerial and financial flexibility (the ability to take advantage of opportunities). It may be feared that the stock market will interpret negatively the substitution of debt for equity.
5. An increase in debt leverage increases the incremental cost of future borrowing.
6. The structure of investor taxes favor the use of some equity (e.g., investors expect future capital gains).

7. Cash flows out of the firm paying the debt interest and principal may restrict growth of the firm.
8. The issuance of debt in substitution for stock may adversely affect EPS.
9. A large part of the burden of bad outcomes falls on management. The increase in compensation to management may not be adequate for management to justify the use of more debt.

All of the above factors are relevant. When the use of more debt seems appropriate, not all decision-makers will be concerned with a negative reaction by the market, but for some managers the market reaction is the primary consideration. Usually management's objectives are more complex than the maximization of expected shareholder value.

Frequently, the economic characteristics of the firm's assets limit the amount of debt (in substitution for stock) that can be issued in the market. However, history shows that lenders will tend to supply incremental debt as long as the expected return for new assets to be financed by the additional debt exceeds the after tax cost of the debt. There is likely to be no practical limit to the amount of debt that can be added to a firm's balance sheet if the firm's asset base can be increased.

Factors Encouraging the Issuance of Debt

There are many valid reasons for corporations to use debt. Among the primary reasons are:

a. Tax deductibility of interest (debt is cheaper after tax than equity thus the use of debt increases the firm's value and reduces its cost of capital).
b. Raise debt capital from banks quickly.
c. Raising equity capital signals overvaluation of the stock so issue debt which signals optimism.
d. Easier to increase ROE (if the investment earns more than the cost of debt). Also may have a desirable effect on EPS.
e. No dilution of voting control of current stockholders.

f. Incentive to management and a constraint of management.
g. Timing (the common stock price is now depressed and capital is needed).
h. Reduces the need for equity capital (using other peoples' money).
i. A large amount of debt tends to discourage raiders.
j. Debt has lower issue costs than new equity.

Tax considerations are very relevant.

The substitution of debt for equity reduces the firm's cost of capital (assuming zero costs of financial distress) and increases the firm's value. It can be readily shown that with zero investor taxes, zero agency costs, and zero costs of financial distress:

$$k_0 = k_e(0)\left(1 - t\frac{B}{V_L}\right) \tag{1}$$

and

$$V_L = V_U + tB \tag{2}$$

where

k_0 is the weighted average cost of capital of a levered firm.
$k_e(0)$ is the cost of equity capital of an unlevered firm.
t is the corporate tax rate.
B is the amount of debt issued in substitution for equity.
V_L is the value of the levered firm.
V_U is the value of the unlevered firm.

Lecture 12

World Prosperity or Economic Chaos?

A look at the big picture. A talk given in Europe in 1991.

Recent research has revealed a very disturbing fact. 60% of those attending this speech will forget what they have heard within 1/2 a day. Despite this fact, I will give my talk.

Eric Severeid, the very respected CBS news analyst of 1940 to 1977, in his retirement speech, offered the advice "not to underestimate the intelligence of the audience and not to overestimate its information."[1]

I neither underestimate the intelligence of the audience nor do I underestimate your information on the subject of my talk. I am sure that collectively you are much better informed than I am. The purpose of my talk is to describe the world economic situation and to raise some economic issues that deserve discussion. Kept hidden, these issues will harm our prosperity. An exposure of the issues may enable us to solve or avoid problems.

There have been three immensely important economic changes in the past forty years. Not listed in order of importance they are: First, the economic and political changes taking place in Eastern Europe and the USSR are the most encouraging events in that part of Europe since the end of World War II in 1945 and the beginning of the Cold War immediately thereafter.

[1] *New York Times*, December 1, 1977, p. 59.

The second important change has been the European Common Market culminating in the changes to take place in 1992. The affluence of Europe today is impressive, but even more important are the changes in trans-nation relationships. These events have changed completely the way that this American views the future of Europe.

The third important change has been economic explosion in the Far East. In less than 45 years Japan has achieved the conquest of Los Angeles, Hawaii, New York, and other U.S. assets by economic means that it failed to achieve by military means. In 30 years, South Korea, largely destroyed by the Korean War, exploited by its Japanese masters until 1945, and with few natural resources, has become an economic giant. Time limitations require that I neglect discussing the outstanding economic progress of Taiwan, China, Thailand, Malaysia, etc.

It has been proven by the Asian countries that the period of time for a country to move from an industrially backward agrarian society to a modern industrial state is very short, less than 30 years.

Large segments of the world population have concluded that freedom and free enterprise lead to more affluence and happier lives. The events of the past seventy years have provided evidence that differences in how economies are organized affect tremendously the effectiveness of these economies. I will go further and suggest that how countries are connected economically (the economic linkages) has a tremendous effect, thus the importance of the Common Market and the new trade agreement between the U.S. and Canada, and the pending agreement between the U.S. and Mexico.

Let me explicitly consider the choices being made:

a. Systems of government and the implied economic system.
b. Extent of reliance on market forces.
c. Relationships of countries (trade agreements).
d. The allocation of resources within a country (Government Spending).

Miss Debbie Solomon said it well. "Make sure you know what you want. Because you're probably going to get it."[2]

I would reword this thought to be "a government or business should make sure its economic incentives are correctly structured, because people will act in accordance with the incentives."

This conclusion applies to profit seeking businesses as well as countries. The economic incentives offered by corporations to its managers and other workers need improvement. U.S. corporations too often reward the mediocrity of top managers.

Last March I listened to a leading French industrialist (Jean Louis Beffe) extoll the praises of that exclusive club, the European Common Market in 1992. He did not describe the effect on the World's non-members. There are currently barriers to trade between the U.S. and the Common Market countries. Tennis players in Europe are subsidizing European suppliers of tennis balls and/or the local tax collector. The changes of 1992 are not aimed at reducing the obstacles to lower priced tennis balls.

My concern is very simple. I remember the Smoot-Hawley tariff law of 1930 and the consequences of that law. Maybe Hitler, the depression of the thirties, and World War II would have occurred without the trade restrictions that took place throughout the world, but there is a temptation to blame (at least partially) the failure of countries to open their borders to the goods of other countries for the bad things that happened from 1930 to 1940.

In 1990, the U.S. has come off of ten years of monstrous trade deficits. The economic consequences are immense and badly understood.

Josef Joffe, foreign editor of a German newspaper, writing in the *New York Times*, states:[3]

> There is a brighter side, consistently overlooked in America — that Uncle Sam may in fact have himself a bargain. Europeans, Japanese and others

---

[2]Debbie K. Solomon, *Cornell Daily Sun,* May 4, 1979.

[3]Josef Joffe, foreign editor of the *Suddeutsche Zeitung*, is author of a book on NATO and burden-sharing.

> continue to finance America's high living standard (by buying up its debt).

I can assure you that Mr. Joffe's logic is not reassuring to me.

While the United States is to a large part responsible for its own problems, trade obstacles are also a factor. Unless the net U.S. trade position improves, there will be substantive actions taken by Congress.

In the past two years, there have been the:

Sale of a LA golf club to the Japanese

Sale of Rockefeller Center

Sale of Columbia Pictures

Sale of RCA Records

Sale of the Public House in Sturbridge Village

Sale of Mamma Leone's

Sale of Pebble Beach Golf courses

A reaction is building up. I stress the fact that this is not just the result of actions by the Japanese, or our other foreign friends. We are also responsible for our fate.

I would like to share with you a few words from George Washington's 1797 farewell address as he relinquished the Presidency:

> Observe good faith and justice toward all nations; cultivate peace and harmony with all ...
>
> ... our commercial policy should hold an equal and impartial hand; neither seeking nor granting exclusive favors nor preferences ...
>
> There can be no greater error than to expect or calculate upon real favors from nation to nation.

Self-interest requires that countries treat other countries with good faith and with an "impartial hand." I see the possibility of a world with countries linked together by economic ties that are more binding than military treaties. A world where resources are devoted to the advancement of the well being of people rather than their destruction. A world where goods are produced in the most efficient environment, and sold without obstacle all over the world.

The alternative vision is a world cut-up into trading blocks with the goods of the wrong country being kept out because their introduction hurts employment or pride. This trading block system and lack of common interests will tend to create conflicts. The conflicts will cause all of us to be somewhat worse off. Protectionism is an international evil, second only to violence. Try to develop a theory of a limited trading group. What is the optimum size of the ECC? What should be the criteria for membership? It is the free trade, not the barriers that give rise to prosperity!

Goya warned us that "The sleep of reason brings forth monsters."[4]

Now the world is changing. Can the U.S. leadership put aside internal politics and self-interests and find the intellectual vision necessary and "reason" for the survival of the United States as one of the great countries of human history? In recent years the U.S. situation has been analogous to that of the man who fell off the top of the Empire State Building. As he passed the twentieth floor he smiled at the watchers and said "So far everything is fine."

I was born in the midst of prohibition, and I was five years old when the stock market crashed in 1929. I spent my childhood and teenage years in the depression. I became an adult in time to participate in World War II and when I was ready to enjoy life, the Korean War caught my attention. It has been a great life, but never has it been better, or the future brighter, for more people of this world than in September 1990. But then, I am not currently standing watch on a U.S. Navy cruiser in the Persian Gulf.

[4]Goya (Los Caprichos).

Lecture 13

How to Invest

This was written and given close to 1987.

Ten Rules for an Investor's Heir*

1. Seek diversification: stocks and other investments. Hold some liquid investments.
2. Your tax situation should influence the mix of investments. Only use complex tax shelters with caution. Only the after-tax return from an investment is relevant.
3. The old adage, "Buy Low, Sell High" is wrong. Never sell a stock voluntarily unless you need cash, a tax loss, your tax situation has changed (see 2), or the market is overpriced (a rare event). "Buy Low" is good advice (but not operational).
4. Never act on advice (a tip) that leads to buying without your checking on the facts. Do basic financial analysis to convince yourself fundamental value lies behind a purchase.
5. The "Greater Fool Theory" is an unreliable basis for betting one's wealth. Look at fundamentals.
6. "Dollar averaging" will ensure that you buy when stock prices are lower than they used to be. It does not increase your expected return. But it is not harmful.
7. Do not buy taxable bonds (for your personal account) above or close to par or maturity value if you are high tax. Preferred stock

*It is assumed you have a healthy aversion to risk.

is not a good investment for a high tax or a low tax investor (OK to consider preferred stock if you are a corporation).

8. Only buy a common stock you expect to hold until your tax or financial situation changes.
9. Do not expect to find experts who can predict the direction of the next market move. Market turns are difficult to predict.
10. Follow the spirit of the first nine rules, not the letter. Do not feel "comfortable" with the stock market or expect to get rich. Remember, there are few "free lunches" in this world, and investments with high potential returns usually are accompanied by high risk.

Question: Were you happy or sad at the end of October 19, 1987?[1]

[1]A day known as "Black Monday", when the Dow Jones Industrial Average dropped 22.6%.

Lecture 14

Dividend Policy

No date and no location but probably near 1990. Probably given in Belgium (based on paper used).

Dividend Growth versus Share Repurchasing

In favor of dividend growth

1. Conventional wisdom is for firms to pay growing dividends (easy to understand).
2. A signal to the market of managerial optimism.
3. Imposes a financial discipline (firm goes to capital market for expansion capital) on management.
4. Stockholders want cash with minimum trouble and cost.
5. Will result in a larger total stock value.

Evaluation of the above

1. While a fact, this is not a valid reason for the action.

2. and 3. Apply equally to share repurchases (thus not listed there).

4. Is valid. But with a dividend, cash is also given to those investors who do not want it.

5. We have no evidence to substantiate this.

In favor of share repurchase

1. An optimal "dividend". Those investors who do not want cash do not sell (save taxes and transaction costs).

2. Taxes:

   a. .28 the capital gains tax rate is less than .396 the tax rate on ordinary income
   b. tax basis of stock is a tax shield
   c. taxes can be deferred

3. Stock price effect:

   a. stock price goes up compared to a cash dividend stock price
   b. stock price goes up (larger EPS)

4. EPS goes up (number of shares goes down).
5. Higher EPS and stock price growth rates.
6. Should increase stock total value. Sooner or later the proposed strategy will impress the stock market.
7. Larger book value (than with dividend).
8. Enhances stock options.

Illustrating the power of share repurchase

1. A firm has $100 of cash.
2. Investor is taxes at .396 on ordinary income and .28 on capital gains.
3. Firm can earn .13 on stock equity capital. Investor can earn $.13(1-.28) = .0936$ after tax.
4. The planning horizon is ten years.

Dividend and then investment

Net of tax $= (1 - .396)100 = \$60.40$
Invest for 10 years $= 60.40(1.0936)^{10} = \$147.78$

Investor retains and sells after ten years

$100(1.13)^{10}(1 - .28) = \$244.41$
A 65% improvement over the dividend.

Same Example: A 20 Year Horizon

Dividend and then investment

$60.40(1.0936)^{20} = \$361.58$

Investor retains and sells after ten years

$100(1.13)^{20}(1 - .28) = \$829.66$
A 129% improvement over the dividend.

Same Example: A One Year Horizon

Dividend and then investment

$60.40(1.0936) = \$66.05$

Investor retains and sells after one year

$100(1.13)(1 - .28) = \$81.36$
A 23% improvement over the dividend.

To Execute the Proposed Strategy There are Four Choices Relative to Dividends

1. Decrease the growth rate in dividends but still grow.
2. Eliminate dividend growth.
3. Decrease the dividend.
4. Eliminate the dividend.

Let us drop (4) from consideration because it would be too drastic a strategy.

To soften the consequences to those investors wanting the cash flow from dividends, they can be given the option of exchanging their common stock for a preferred stock that pays a higher dividend than the common. This alternative deserves consideration.

Lecture 15

An Investment and Financial Restructuring Strategy

I was thinking of these issues in late 1989. I gave several talks to an investment bank during this time period.

An Investment and Financial Restructuring Strategy

Problems:

1. It is very difficult to beat the Standard and Poor 500 Index consistently.
2. It is very difficult to earn an excess return consistently by a conventional investment strategy.

Solution:

Make investments with the objective of restructuring the firms.

There is value added.

Other problems:

1. Market may go down (can hedge this).
2. Company's stock may go down because of major corporate operating problem (this is a major risk).
3. The restructuring does not take place because of effective opposition (this is a major risk).
4. Bad public relations (despite the fact that everyone can benefit).

Note: The logic also applies to a corporation wanting to increase shareholder value.

Objective of Lecture

Show that value is added by substituting debt for equity if there is debt capacity. An investor will earn the same return as without the debt, but will have extra "free" cash to invest.

A general solution will be derived using the following set of symbols and will be illustrated using numerical examples.

Financial Strategy: The Use of Debt Delevering with Taxes

Symbols to be Used:

p	fraction of unlevered firm purchased
V_u	value of unlevered firm
V_L	value of levered firm
t	corporate tax rate
X	earnings before taxes and before new interest
S	value of stock after issuance of debt
B	value of debt issued
I	interest on new debt issued
$(1 - t)p$	fraction of new debt purchased
$k_e(0)$	cost of equity with zero debt
$k_e(L)$	cost of equity with debt

The no-tax situation

Unlevered Firm

pV_u	is value of firm owned by investor
pX	is earnings before interest by investor

Levered Firm

Substitute B of debt for B of stock. Investors buys p of debt and p of stock.

pS earns	p(X − I)
pB earns	pI
Sum	pX

The same return is earned as with the unlevered firm; therefore

$$pV_u = pB + pS$$

or

$$V_u = B + S$$

The firm's value is not affected by the substitution.

Example

$E(X) = \$1{,}000{,}000, V_u = \$10{,}000{,}000, k_e(0) = .10$ Assume the investor owns 20% or $200,000.

Levered Firm

Now substitute $8,000,000 of debt paying .07 interest or $560,000 per year. The investor buys 20% of the debt and 20% of the stock.

pS earns	.2(1,000,000 − 560,000)
pB earns	.2(560,000)
Sum	$200,000

The value is V_L =	$1,000,000
B =	800,000
S	$ 200,000

$$\frac{1{,}000{,}000 - 560{,}000}{k_e(L)} = 200{,}000$$

$$k_e(L) = .4545$$

The corporate tax situation

We want to show that

$$V_L = V_u + tB$$

We will only assume that a given cash flow stream has one value.

tB is the value added by substituting debt for equity.

If B = $1,000,000,000 and if t = .35, the value added by the substitution of debt for equity is:

$$tB = .35(1{,}000{,}000{,}000) = \$350{,}000{,}000.$$

Can value be added by merely substituting debt or equity?

Note: It will be assumed that there are no costs of financial distress (for simplicity of presentation).

Financial strategy: The use of debt

<u>With No New Debt</u>

Buy p of the stock of unlevered firm (V_u)
Investment of pV_u
Earn: p(l-t)X

<u>With New Debt</u>

Buy same percentage p of stock and p(l-t) of the debt:

pS of stock and earn	$p(1 - t)(X - I)$
$p(1 - t)B$ of debt and earn	$p(1 - t)I$
Sum =	$p(1 - t)X$

The same return is earned <u>and</u> the cost (investment) must be the same as the unlevered firm.

With equal investments:

$$pV_u = pS + p(1 - t)B$$

Since $V_L = S + B$:

$$pV_u + ptB = p(S + B) = pV_L$$

Dividing by p:

$$V_L = V_u + tB.$$

The value of the unlevered firm is increased by tB.

Assume:
$X = \$200{,}000, t = .35, p = .25, (1 - t)X = \$130{,}000, B = \$800{,}000, k_i = .15, I = \$120{,}000$

<u>Unlevered Firm</u>

$X(1 - t) =$	\$130,000
The Investor Owns .25:	x .25
Investor Earns	\$ 32,500

<u>Levered Firm</u>

$$(X - I)(1 - t) = (200{,}000 - 120{,}000)(1 - .35) = \$\ 52{,}000$$

$$I = \$120{,}000$$

The investor earns:

Interest: $.25(1 - .35)120{,}000 =$	\$19,500
Stock: $\$52{,}000(.25) =$	13,000
Investor Earns	\$32,500

Assume the firm has a bad year and only earns:

$$X = \$120{,}000$$

<u>Unlevered Firm</u>

$X(1 - t) = 120{,}000(1 - .35) =$	\$78,000
	x .25
Investor Earns	\$19,500

Levered Firm

Stock return is zero	
Interest	\$120,000
The Investor Earns:	
\$120,000(.25)(1 − .35) =	\$ 19,500

The returns will always be equal with the special vertical slice strategy (buying both the stock and the debt).

Value Added: Making Money

$X = \$200{,}000, t = .35, k_e(0) = .20, p = .25$

Unlevered Firm (No Growth)

$$V_u = \frac{(1 - .35)200,000}{.20} = \$650{,}000$$

Percentage of Ownership	x .25
Value of Investment	\$162,500

Levered Firm

Substitute \$800,000 of debt (note \$800,000 > \$660,000).
$k_i = .15, B = \$800,000, p = .25$
$V_L = V_u + tB = 650{,}000 + .35(800{,}000) = 650{,}000 + 280{,}000 = \$930{,}000$
$B = \$800{,}000, I = \$120{,}000, S = \$130{,}000$
since:
$V_L = S + B = 130{,}000 + 800{,}000 = \$930{,}000.$
We can solve for the implied equity cost with debt:

$$\frac{(1 - .35)(200{,}000 - 120{,}000)}{k_e(L)} = 130{,}000$$

$k_e(L) = .40$

Adding Value

1. Issue \$800,000 of debt paying .15.
2. Pay the \$800,000 from the debt to stockholders (\$800,000 × .25 = \$200,000 to the investor).

3. Investor buys .1625 of the debt and .25 of stock:

.25(1 − .35)(800,000) of debt =	\$130,000
Investment in debt	\$130,000
Common Stock Investment	32,500
Free Value	70,000
New Value for Investor	\$232,500

Would you rather have \$162,500 or \$232,500? Can also add real value from real changes.

The value added (with zero tax investors) can be as large as .54 of initial value.

$$\text{Value Added} = t_c B = \frac{t_c}{1 - t_c} V_u = \frac{.35}{.65} V_u = .54 V_u.$$

Since $V_u = \$650{,}000$, the maximum value that can be added is:
Value Added = .35(650,000) = \$350,000.
Assume \$1,000,000 of debt is issued:
$V_L = 650{,}000 + .35(1{,}000{,}000) = \$1{,}000{,}000$
$B = \$1{,}000{,}000, S = \$0$
Maximum debt = \$1,000,000.

Also:

a. Maximum Debt$= \dfrac{X}{k_e(0)} = \dfrac{200{,}000}{.20} = \$1{,}000{,}000$
b. Note that Interest must not be larger than EBIT = \$200,000.

A Summary of the Process

1. Identify companies with large tax payments (large taxable income) and relatively small amount of debt.
2. Let

V_u	be value of firm before restructuring
$E(X)$	be expected earnings before interest and taxes
$k_e(0)$	be the cost of equity with zero tax

We want:

$$V_L = V_u + t(V_L)$$

or

$$\mathrm{V_L} = \frac{V_u}{1-t}, \text{ is the maximum debt}$$

Since

$$\mathrm{V_u} = \frac{\mathrm{E(X)(1-t)}}{\mathrm{k_e(0)}}$$

$$\text{Maximum debt} = \frac{\mathrm{E(X)}}{\mathrm{k_e(0)}}$$

Determine the amount of debt to be issued (B), where B is less than the maximum debt.

3. tB is the value added.
4. It is required that

   Taxable Income $\geq \mathrm{k_i B}$

   where $\mathrm{k_i}$ is interest rate
   B is debt issue

   Taxable income is before the new debt is issued.

Lecture 16

Long-Term Financial Planning Goals

Some basic rules.

Long-Term Financial Planning and Setting Goals

Financial planning

a. Trade-offs between incremental consumption now, consumption later, or leaving wealth for heirs.
b. Allocating resources defined as savings between types of assets.

Setting goals

a. The minimum amounts needed for life's predictable crises (or challenges) should be defined.
b. Amounts in excess of the minimums needed should depend on circum-stances.

Investing Strategies

First line of defense

$$\text{Income} - \text{Consumption} = \text{Savings}$$

Conclusion:
Make money
Control consumption consistent with savings goals.

Before investing in securities

Buy a residence
Adequate insurance
Working capital (cash)

Primary investing vehicles

Pension funds — 401k, etc.
Keogh Plans, IRA's
May have to borrow to participate.

Assume you do not have the $1,000 for 401k. Borrow at a cost of .10 before tax and .10(1−.396)=.0604 after tax (home equity loan, not credit cards). With borrowing (a−10 year horizon horizon) we have:

Time 0	Time 10
Loan +1,000	−1,797.62 Loan payment (after tax)
Payment −1,000	
Tex Saving +396	+711.86 Tax Saving Compounded at .0604
Value of Pension $1{,}000(1.10)^{10}$	+2.593.74 or $ 1,566.62 after tax
Value Added for $1,000 borrowed	+$1,507.98
	or $ 480.86 after tax

Conclusions

Pay a maximum amount into pension plans (a defined contribution plan) if you are paying taxes.

a. Save taxes at time of payment.
b. Accumulate on a tax free basis.

Assume There is Extra Cash

The alternatives are:

a. Mutual funds
   Advantages:

Diversification
Expert management
Ease
Disadvantages:
Cost
Turnover: Realization of capital gains.

b. Common Stock
c. Preferred stock (competing with corporate buyers)
d. Special Preferreds — PERCS
e. Debt
   Corporate (AAA to BB)
   Tax Exempts
   Treasuries (Bills to 30 year Strips)
   CD's
   Two risk dimensions:
      a. Credit risk
      b. Interest rate risk
f. Exotic alternatives:
      Vacation home(s)
      Art, stamp, coins
      Cornell University

Tax Strategies

Preferred stock (e.g. PERCS), high dividend common, and debt should be in tax protected vehicles.

Capital gain common can be help outside of tax protected vehicles.

Pension funds should be "managed" since they can become too large.

Tax strategies include:

a. Keogh Plan, 401k, etc.
b. Tax exempt bonds.
c. Gifts to children (spread income).
d. Some non-dividend paying common stocks.

e. Buy real assets (stamps, art, coins, land, games, etc.). Distinguish between gambling and investing.
f. Buy and manage real estate (ugh!).
g. Tax sheltered earnings (options, deferred pay).

Common Stocks

Three issues

a. Extent of diversification.
b. Which stock?
c. What allocation?

Diversification

Consider the following table showing "Risk Reduction".

With 10 securities you reduce 90% of the risk that can be reduced!

With 100 securities you reduce 99% of the risk that can be reduced.

However, you reduce more risk if the securities have a relatively low correlation (connection).

Risk Reduction

Portfolio variance as fraction of individual security variance

Number of Securities in the Portfolio	Correction Between Securities (r)					Percent of Max Risk Reduction
	1.0	0.8	0.5	0.1	0	$\frac{N-1}{N}$
1	1.0	1.0	1.0	1.0	1.0	0
2	1.0	0.9	0.75	0.55	0.50	1/2
10	1.0	0.82	0.55	0.19	0.10	9/10
100	1.0	0.802	0.505	0.109	0.01	99/100
∞	1.0	0.800	0.500	0.100	0.00	1

When can risk be reduced to zero?

Which Stock?

What company should you invest in?

a. Do you know a good person heading a corporation you would like to invest in?
b. Do you know a product that is so good you want to invest in the firm?
c. Do you know a firm whose style (concept) you like?

What industry? What firm in that industry?

a. Use your special (not inside) information.
b. Diversify.

Note: There can be a good firm with a good product, but it is a bad common stock investment (the stock price is too high) or the firm has "bad luck".

Conclusion: Diversify.

Investments: Analysis of Common Stock

The following information is of interest:

a. Current market price
b. Dividend yield (past 12 months and history through time)
c. Current price/earnings ratio
d. Past market prices and fluctuations and forecast of future
e. Relationship to other investments
f. Earnings, current, past, and future
g. Nature of the company's business, recent developments and future prospects, products and markets, practices
h. Most recent quarterly results (earnings)
i. Balance sheet data: current ratio, debt/equity, etc.
j. Interest coverage (times earned)
k. Hidden liabilities (pension, leases, etc.)
l. Accounting practices (LIFO, depreciation, etc.)
m. Growth rates of earnings, dividends, etc.

n. Book value
o. Which market is it traded on? Liquidity of securities
p. Strategy, operating and financial decisions of firm
q. Capital structure
r. Managerial compensation practices

The Allocation

The allocation between stock and other investments, including cash.

We know that for any 30 year time period since 1926, you are better off holding common stock than other security.

However, there are some (20) years in which the return from holding common stock is negative and additional years when stock did not do as well as debt.

We know that we cannot pick the moment of maximum stock market level nor determine when the market has reached a bottom.

We are not good allocating investments.

However, based on past history, one should be 100% in stock if you believe history repeats itself, and you will hold the investment for at least 30 years after the worst market collapse.

With less certain beliefs, you should not have 100% of your savings in stocks.

Conclusions

1. Diversify.
2. Taxes (institutional factors) are relevant.
3. Markets are relatively efficient.
4. Basic analysis is useful.
5. Do not rely on someone dumber than you to bale you out.
6. Beware "rules of thumb" without theory.
7. Market turns are difficult to predict.
8. There are risk and return trade-offs.
9. The stock market throughout history has been a "fair gamble" and you should always own some stock.

   The casino in Ledyard offers "unfair" gambles.

Strategies that can Lead to Maximum Returns (and Maximum Losses)

1. Buy one "best" stock.
2. Buy one "best" call option.
3. Buy stock market index futures.
4. Use debt to do any of the above.
5. Some funds use preferred stock for leverage.
6. Sell "puts" (and have stocks go up).
7. Own no stocks (and have stocks go down and stay down).

Wall Street Trends, Booms, and Crashes

All of the above are predictable after they happen.

Is the market too high?

Consider a stock price of $200:

$$P = \frac{10}{.10 - .05} = \$200.$$

Now assume the cost of equity goes to .07.

$$P = \frac{10}{.07 - .05} = \$500.$$

This is a rational boom (all things equal).

Common Stock Dividends and Capital Gains

Assume:

Capital gains tax rate = .20
Ordinary income tax rate = .396
Return (after tax) investors can earn = .0604
Return corporation can earn = .10
Investment horizon = 15 years
Corporation has $100 that it can invest or pay a dividend.

Dividend

Investor nets \$60.40:

$$60.40(1.0604)^{15} = \$145.57$$

Retention and then Capital Gain

$$100(1.1)^{15}(1 - .20) = \$334.18$$

If investors can earn .08 the \$100 dividend will grow to:

$$100(1 - .396)(1.08)^{15} = \$191.60$$

Even if the \$100 at time 0 results in a capital gain we only have:

$$100(1 - .20)(1.08)^{15} = \$253.77$$

which is again less than \$334.18.

Conclusion

If you have a long time horizon (over a year) buy the stock of companies that are not paying a dividend (and are growing).

Reinvested earnings are powerful.

We want to compare

a. Dividends
b. Retention
c. DRIP (dividend reinvestment plan)

Retention is preferred.

A DRIP offers low cost reinvesting but the dividends-reinvested are taxed and there may be some transaction costs. May be better than dividends.

Dividends are third, unless you want (or need) immediate cash.

Lecture 17

High Priority Corporate Finance Issues Circa 1990

This paper is a good summary of corporate finance theory and practice in 1990.

The Johnson Graduate School of Management Life Long Learning: High Priority Corporate Finance Issues

1. An overview of corporate finance in the 1990's.
2. Financial engineering strategies.
3. Capital structure considerations.
4. Dividend policy with President Clinton.
5. NPV (Uncertainty and the discount rate).
6. Measuring performance (Economic income).

Topic 1: An Overview of Corporate Finance in the 1990s

1. S&L's and Drexel[1] out of junk bond market.
2. Temporary shrinkage of investment banks and corporate finance groups of commercial banks.
3. Reduced threat of LBO's and M&A.
   But we can expect:

[1]Drexel Burnham, a famous and infamous investment bank.

4. Proxy fights and common stock offers.
5. Pension funds looking aggressively for higher returns and boards will exercise more power.
6. Foreign capital.
7. The tax law changes (higher tax rates) will increase the value of financial engineering.
8. Acquisitions by giant firms will continue (AT&T and NCR).
9. Restructurings (Divestments) and Bankruptcies.
10. Surprises will happen.

Topic 2: Financial Engineering Strategies

Three types of financial strategies

1. Motivated by institutional factors (e.g. taxes and regulations).
2. Real (affect assets and liabilities independent of institutional factors).
3. Magic.

Type 1: Motivated by institutional factors

a. Substitution of debt for equity (capital structure).
b. Utilization of share repurchase.
c. Substitution of retention for dividends.
d. Exchange offers (debt and/or preferred stock for common).
e. Rapid payments into the pension fund.
f. Mergers and acquisitions (see Type 2).
g. Investment in common stocks of other firms (e.g. Berkshire-Hathaway's strategy).

The above can be "dressed up" by using convertibles, zeros, etc., but tax-strategy normally generates the value.

These strategies are most important for firms with incomes.

Type 2: Real

a. Reasonable evaluation of investments (capital budgeting).
b. Buy versus lease decisions.

c. Refunding of high cost debt.
d. Congruent performance measurement and good investment policies.
e. Mergers and acquisitions.
f. Working capital decisions (inventories, credit, etc.).
g. Risk management.

Type 3: Magic

These strategies rely on someone being fooled (a greater fool theory of finance).

a. Letter or tracking stock.
   Sum of the parts is worth more than the whole. (RJR Nabisco)
b. Dividend reinvestment plans.
c. A high P/E firm acquiring a low P/E firm.
d. Decisions for accounting effects (operating leases are off the balance sheet).
e. Stock dividends.

Topic 3: Capital Structure — Corporate Taxes But No Investor Taxes

Let t be the corporate tax rate.

It can be shown that:

$$\text{Value of Levered Firm} = \text{Value of Unlevered Firm} + \text{t (New Debt)}$$

or

$$V_L = V_u + tB$$

and

$$\text{Maximum Value Added} = \frac{t}{1-t} V_u$$

If $t = .36$ then $\frac{.36}{1-.36} = .5625$:

Maximum Value Added = .5625 V_u and $V_L = 1.5625\ V_u$.

Conclusion: Value can be increased by a maximum of .5625 if assumptions are valid. Other changes can increase value more.

Example: t = .36, No growth, Cost of capital = .20.

Earnings before interest and taxes = $200,000

Earnings after taxes with equity = $(1 - .36)200,000 = \$128,000$

The Unlevered Firm has a value of:

$$V_u = \frac{128,000}{.20} = \$640,000$$

Now substitute $800,000 of .15 debt for common stock (note $800,000 is larger than $640,000).

$$\text{Interest} = .15(800,000) = \$120,000$$

The investors now earn:

Stock (200,000 – 120,000)(1 – .36)=	$ 51,200
Debt	120,000
Total earnings	$171,200

$$\begin{aligned} V_L = V_u + tB &= 640,000 + .36(800,000) \\ &= 640,000 + 288,000 = \$928,000 \end{aligned}$$

Compare $928,000 and $640,000 (values)
$171,200 and $128,000 (earnings).

A special strategy

Buy all the stock and (1–t) of the new debt.

The investor earns $128,000 with all equity firm.

The investor earns with the $800,000 debt firm:

Stock investment earns	$ 51,200
Debt earns (1–.36)120,000	76,800
	$128,000

The earnings are identical.

Conclusion:

There is an investment strategy that will cause the return from a highly levered firm to be identical to the return from an all equity firm.

Note:

There are costs of financial distress.

Adding value to a firm with an initial value of $640,000

1. Issue $800,000 of debt paying .15.
2. Pay the $800,000 from the debt to stockholders.
3. Investor buys (1−.36)(800,000) of debt = $512,000

Investment in debt	$512,000
Common Stock Investment	128,000
Free Value	288,000
New Value for Investor	$928,000

Would you rather have $640,000 or $928,000?

Can also add real value from real changes.

The value added (with zero tax investors) can be as large as .5625 of initial value.

$$\text{Maximum Value Added} = \frac{\text{t}}{1-\text{t}}\text{V}_\text{u} = \frac{.36}{.64} = .5625\text{V}_\text{u}$$

Issue $1,000,000 of debt.

$$\text{V}_\text{L} = \text{V}_\text{u} + \text{tB} = 640,000 + 360,000 = \$1,000,000$$

$$\text{Maximum Value Added} = \frac{360,000}{640,000} = .5625.$$

Note: Must be able to use tax deductions.

Can buy all \$800,000 of the debt (receive \$171,200 rather than \$128,000 per year).

Implications for top management

Financial engineering strategies can add value, thus should be considered, but beware of "magic". Financial engineering that adds value can be explained.

The real financial strategies can affect the very existence of the firm. Investment strategies must be evaluated in a theoretically correct manner (method and discount rates).

Appendix: Financial Strategy — the Use of Debt Symbols to Be Used

V_u	value of unlevered firm
V_L	value of levered firm
t	corporate tax rate
X	earnings before taxes and before new interest
S	value of stock after issuance of debt
B	value of debt issued
I	interest on new debt issued
$(1 - t)$	fraction of new debt purchased

We want to show that

$$V_L = V_u + tB$$

We will only assume that a given cash flow stream has a given value.

tB is the value added by substituting debt for equity.

Financial Strategy: The Use of Debt Delevering With Taxes

<u>With No New Debt</u>

Buy the stock of firm (V_u)

Investment of V_u
Earn: $(1 - t)X$

<u>With New Debt</u>

Buy same percentage of stock and (1-t) of debt:	
S of stock and earn	(1-t)(X-1)
(1-t)B of debt and earn	(1-t)1
Sum =	(1-t)X

The same return is earned <u>and</u> the cost (investment) must be the same as the unlevered firm.

With equal investments:

$$V_u = S + (1 - t)B$$

Since $V_L = S + B$:

$$V_u + tB = (S + B) = V_L$$

and

$$V_L = V_u + tB$$

Topic 4: Dividend Policy

Alternatives:

1. Retention
2. Cash dividend
3. DRIP
4. Share repurchase

An Example:

Consider Corporation A with \$1,000. $t_p = .396$, $t_g = .28$. Stock Tax Basis = \$1,000

	Investor	Corporation A
Retention	\$ 1,000 of stock	\$1,000 of cash
Cash dividend	\$ 604 of cash	zero cash
DRIP	\$ 1,000 of stock –\$ 396 of cash	\$1,000 of cash
Share repurchase	\$ 1,000 of cash*	zero cash

*With a zero tax basis, the \$1,000 cash would be \$720.

Share Repurchase

1. $t_p = .396$, $t_g = .28$. Differential. Tax basis protection.
2. Stock price effects (100,000 shares outstanding)

Value before "dividend"	\$5,000,000	\$50 per share
Dividend	1,000,000	
Value after dividend	\$4,000,000	\$40 per share

With repurchase of 20,000 shares:

$$\frac{\$4,000,000}{80,000} = \$50.$$

3. Cosmetics.
4. Optional dividend (transaction costs, taxes).
5. Stock options.

Topic 5: Capital Budgeting Uncertainty and the Discount Rate

When can $(1 + r)^{-n}$ be used?

Constant risk aversion: A definition

Let

$\bar{X}$ be the expected cash flow

CE be the certainty equivalent

$$j = \frac{\bar{X}}{CE} \tag{1}$$

If j is constant for all time periods and all values of $\bar{X}$, then there is constant risk aversion.

An example of a certainty equivalent

Let there be uncertainty where the gamble has a value of \$454.545:

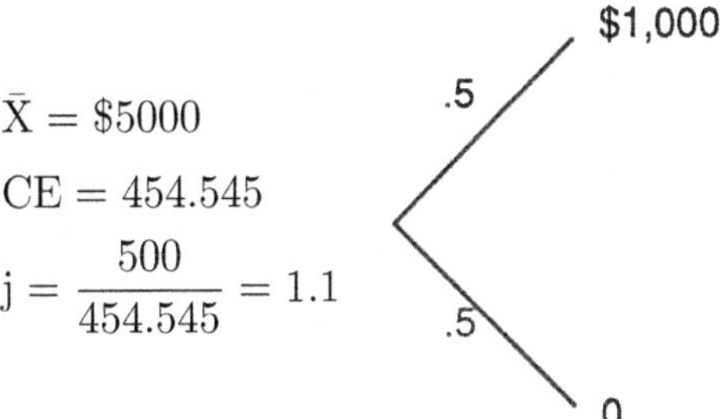

Time discounting

Assume that an investment's expected cash flows are discounted using a risk adjusted discounted rate (r_n). If $\bar{X}$ is received at time n, the present value (PV) is:

$$PV = \bar{X}(1 + r_n)^{-n} = \frac{\bar{X}}{(1 + r_n)^n} \tag{2}$$

The CE can be discounted using the risk free rate (r_f) since the CE is equivalent in value to a certain cash flow. For the present value we have

$$PV = CE(1 + r_f)^{-n} = \frac{CE}{(1 + r_f)^n} \tag{3}$$

Equating the values of equations (2) and (3):

$$\bar{X}(1 + r_n)^{-n} = CE(1 + r_f)^{-n} \tag{4}$$

Table 1: Constant Values of j and r_f.

Values of r_n if $j = 1.10$, $r_f = .04$

Time: n	$(j)^{\frac{1}{n}}$	$1 + r_f$	$r_n = (1 + r_f)(j)^{\frac{1}{n}} - 1$
1	1.1000	1.04	.144
2	1.04881	1.04	.09076
3	1.0323	1.04	.074
5	1.0192	1.04	.060
10	1.0096	1.04	.050
15	1.0064	1.04	.047
20	1.0048	1.04	.045
50	1.0010	1.04	.041

Since $j = \dfrac{\bar{X}}{CE}$ and $j(CE) = \bar{X}$, substituting in (4) we obtain:

$$j(1 + r_n)^{-n} = (1 + r_f)^{-n}$$

and

(5) $$j = \left(\frac{1 + r_n}{1 + r_f}\right)^n$$

If $r_n = .144$ and $r_f = .04$ and $n = 1$:

$$j = \frac{1.144}{1.04} = 1.10$$

If $n = 2$, then $j = 1.21$.

If r_n and r_f are constant for different values of n then it implies j increases through time. But if j and r_f are held constant then the discount rate for a cash flow at time $n(r_n)$ is:

(6) $$r_n = (1 + r_f)j^{\frac{1}{n}} - 1$$

Remember that $\bar{X}$ is an expectation and only adjusts for risk aversion. Table 1 shows that r_n decreases as n increases and that r_n approaches r_f as n becomes large.

Continuing the example

Let C be the cost of the gamble.

Assume $r_f = .04$, $n = 1$, $r_1 = .144$, $C = \$400.00$

(2) $$PV = \frac{\bar{X}}{(1+r_1)^n} = \frac{500}{1.144} = \$437.06$$

(3) $$PV = \frac{CE}{(1+r_f)^n} = \frac{454.545}{1.04} = \$437.06$$

The internal rate of return of the investment is:

$$500(1+r)^{-1} = 400.00$$

$$r = .25$$

Now assume the same outcomes are at $n = 2$.

(2) $$PV = \frac{\bar{X}}{(1+r_2)^2} = \frac{500}{(1.09076)^2} = \$420.25$$

(3) $$PV = \frac{CE}{(1+r_f)^2} = \frac{454.545}{(1.04)^2} = \$420.25$$

Using the .144 as the discount rate:

$$PV = \frac{\bar{X}}{(1+r)^2} = \frac{500}{(1.144)^2} = \$382.05$$

Should the investor pay \$400 for this investment?

The first two computations indicate yes and the third (with a present value of \$382.05 and a negative NPV) indicates no.

If \$400 is borrowed at a cost of .04 (the default free rate) then \$432.64 would be owed. But the gamble could be sold for its certainty equivalent of \$454.545, thus the loan is risk free.

The .144 is too high a discount rate for $n = 2$.

Topics 6: Measuring Managerial Performance

Some alternatives

Quantitative Measures of "Profits"

a. Operating Margins
 Percentages

Dollar Amounts

b. ROI or ROE or ROA
c. Economic Income (residual income)
d. Earnings per share (for a period of years)
e. Stockholder Returns (market inputs)

Other considerations:

a. Present growth and foundation for future growth
b. Qualitative factors
c. Other goals (sales, share of market, risk)

Conclusion:

We cannot measure managerial performance, but must do so anyway.

ROE, ROI, ROA, Operating Margins, CFROGI all have major deficiencies, but can contribute to an impression.

The best single measure is

Economic Income (residual income)

Economic Income

Definition

Income after tax after depreciation after an interest cost of all capital used.

Advantages

a. Any investment with a positive Net Present Value or an Internal Rate of Return larger than the required return will have economic incomes with the same net present value.
b. Will tend to not affect adversely investment or divestment decisions.
c. Management is charged for the capital it uses.

Complexities

a. A year's income may be unsatisfactory, but the investment desirable.
b. Risk differentials (different lived assets).
c. Changing interest rates.

Example: Economic Income

The firm has a .10 cost of money

Time	Expected Cash Flows
0	−3,000
1	+1,500
2	+1,300
3	+1,200

Economic Incomes:

	Year 1	Year 2	Year 3
Revenues	1,500	1,300	1,200
Depreciation	1,000	1,000	1,000
Income	500	300	200
Interest	300	200	100
Economic Income	200	100	100

$$\text{NPV} = -3,000 + \frac{1,500}{1.10} + \frac{1,300}{1.21} + \frac{1,200}{1.331} = \$339.59$$

$$\text{PV of Economic Income} = \frac{200}{1.10} + \frac{100}{1.21} + \frac{100}{1.331} = \$339.59$$

What happens if the firm invests in a project earning less than .10? More than .10?

What happens if the firm earns more than $1,500 in year one?

One Remaining Problem

What happens if cash flows start out relatively slowly?

Needed: A better method of measuring investment and income and depreciation expense.

Lecture 18

Investing in an Uncertain World

This was written close to 1990. May have been given in Canada.

What do the following dates have in common?

a. October 24, 1929
b. October 19, 1987
c. October 13, 1989

Question: In what year would you earn the highest annual return by investing in stocks?

Answer: 54% in year ________.

Chart 1: Federal Reserve Board's index of industrial production, adjusted for seasonal variations. Monthly average, 1923–1925 — 100.

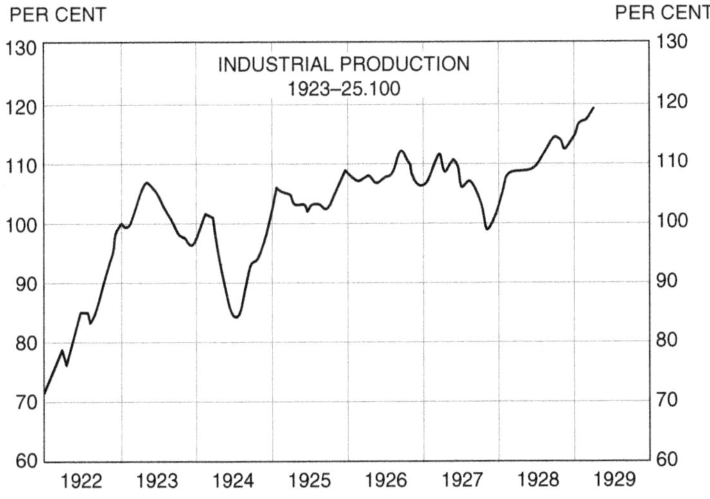

The 1929 Stock Market Crash

Table 1: Index of Stock Market Value

Year	Index of Value	Change in Index	Percentage Change
1925	1.000		
1926	1.057	.057	+5.7%
1927	1.384	.327	+30.9
1928	1.908	.524	+37.9
1929	1.681	−.224	−11.9
1930	1.202	−.479	−28.5
1931	.636	−.434	−36.1
1932	.540	−.096	−15.1
1933	.792	+.252	+46.7

Growth In Corporate Earnings

Third Quarter, 1929	14.1% growth
Nine Months, 1929	20.3% growth

Why Did DJIA Fall In October 1987?

1. Twin deficits
   $175\text{B}(8.10)(1.10)^8 = 933.61(1.10)^8 = 2{,}001.$
   Pay $200.1 billion per year for ever!
2. Exchange rates: devaluation
3. Interest rates up
4. Government talk of not allowing interest as deduction (for M & A's)
5. Program Trading
   Portfolio Insurance

"The lower the stock, the more we sell."

6. High P/E's. 20 in NYSE
   75 in Tokyo

7. Ratio of bond yields to stock yields.
8. Market was too high.
9. We do not know.

Investment Period Returns (1926–1987)

Period	Number of Negative Returns	Number of Periods Less Than 5%
1 year	19	
5	7	
10	2	8
20	0	3+

*There were no periods less than 3.11% return.

DAMET

D for Diversification
A for Analysis or Allocation
M for Market Turns (cannot predict)
E for Efficient Markets (do not go in and out)
T for Tax considerations

Conclusions

1. Diversify
2. Taxes (institutional factors) are relevant
3. Markets are relatively efficient
4. Basic analysis is useful
5. Do not rely on someone dumber than you to bale you out
6. Beware "rules of thumb" without theory
7. Market turns are difficult to predict
8. There are risk and return trade-offs

Remember

1. The future is uncertain.
2. Many things we know are not so.
3. Not all stock market crashes are deserved. Few are explained satisfactorily. All are predicted. More are predicted than occur.
4. Not all crashes are harmful for very long.
5. DAMET.

Lecture 19

Financial Strategies in Uncertain Times

This was a talk given in New York to Cornell University alumni and guests.

Objective of Lecture

Communicate the hypotheses that:

a. financial strategies can significantly affect shareholder value.
b. the process of uncertainty does not affect this conclusion.

How Does One Increase the Value of a Firm Through Finance?

a. Capital Budgeting
b. Capital structure
c. Dividend policy
d. Other

Capital Budgeting

a. The choice of the discount rate(s)
b. Valuing real options
c. Buy versus lease decisions

d. Performance measurement consistent with good investment policies
e. Risk Management

Capital Structure

With no costs of financial distress it can be shown that:

$$V_L = V_u + tB$$

where

V_L is the value of the levered firm
V_u is the value of the unlevered firm
t is the corporate tax rate
B is the debt that is added in substitution of common stock equity.

With maximum debt and $t = .35$ we have

$$V_L = \frac{V_u}{1-t} = 1.54\ V_u$$

Value can be increased by 54%.

But there are complexities:

a. Investor taxes
b. Costs of financial distress (including an inability of the firm to execute real plans).
c. Effect of debt issuance on EPS.
d. Stockholders benefit, but CEO incurs the cost. Today there is little or no incentive for a firm to increase the percentages of debt.

Dividend versus Retained Earnings

Investor earns .064 (tax rate is .36).
Corporation earns .10
A fifteen year horizon.

With a \$100 dividend and then investment for 15 years.

$$(1 - .36)100(1.064)^{15} = \$162$$

With retention:

$$100(1.10)^{15} = \$418$$

With retention and then a capital gains taxed at .18:

$$100(1.10)^{15}(1 - .18) = \$343$$

Value is more than doubled by retention. Also, there are the savings of the other fourteen years.

Debt or common stock?

	Dept	Common Stock	Retained Earnings
EBIT	\$100	\$100	\$100
Interest or Dividend	100	100	
Corporate Tax	0	0	35
Investor Tax	36	36	—
Net	\$64	\$64	\$65*

*There will be a tax to investor when the stock is sold.

Dividend or share repurchase?

Consider a share repurchase. There is \$35 of corporate tax. The cash flow to investors is \$65 but this is taxed ($t_g = .20$).

With more than \$65 of the basis the investor nets more than \$65.

With \$65 of tax basis the investor nets \$65.

With \$0 of tax basis the investor nets $.8(65) = \$52$.

Dividends give \$64. Dividends tend to win.

$t_p = .36$ but t_p is reduced to Zero for Dividends

$t_c = .35$

No change in corporate taxes

	Debt	Common Stock (Dividend)	Common Stock (Retention)	Common Stock (Share Repurchase)
EBIT	$100	$100	$100	$100
Corporate Tax	0	35	35	35
Investor Tax	36	0	0	Some Tax
Net	$64	$65	$65*	Less than $65

1. Common stock beats debt
2. Dividend is as good as retention
3. Dividend beats share repurchase

*There is some tax in the future

Assume Tax on Dividends is Reduced to .20.

$t_g = .20$.

	Debt	Common Stock (Dividend)	Common Stock (Retention)	Common Stock (Share Repurchase)
EBIT	$100	$100	$100	$100
Corporate Tax	0	35	35	35
Investor Tax	36	13*	0**	0**
Net	$64	$52	$65	$65

*Dividend is $65.

**The tax in the future may be as high as .20(65) = $13. But this amount must be time discounted.

Dividends are almost as good as other common stock alternatives, but still inferior.

Share Repurchase versus Dividends

Ordinary income tax rate = .36

Capital gains tax rate = .18

Price = Tax Basis = $20 per share

$200,000 available. 100,000 shares (investor owns 1,000 shares).

Cash Dividends

Investor receives $\$2 \times 1,000 =$	$\$2,000$
Tax (.36)	-720
	$1,280

Share Repurchase

Investor sells 100 shares

Investor receives $100 \times 20 = \$2,000$

(no tax, no taxable gain)

Stock Price Effect (Initial Price = $20)

Common Stock Value	$2,000,000
less (repurchase)	–200,000
New Value	$1,800,000

After dividend:

$$\mathrm{P} = \frac{1,800,000}{100,000} = \$18$$

After share repurchase (10,000 shares)

$$\mathrm{P} = \frac{1,800,000}{90,000} = \$20 \text{ (no change)}$$

But through time with Div equal to 10% of market capitalization the price will grow at:

$$g = \frac{\text{Div}}{\text{V} - \text{Div}} = \frac{200,000}{2,000,000 - 200,000} = 0.l11$$

Assumes zero real growth.

$$\mathrm{P}_1 = \frac{2,000,000}{90,000} = \$22.22$$

At time 10, the stock price can be expected to be:

$$\mathrm{P}_{10} = 20(1.111)^{10} = \$57.30$$

Share Repurchase

1. Stock price effect
2. EPS effect (and other cosmetic changes)
3. Firm buys undervalued stock
4. Partial LBO
5. Tax effects for investor (tax deferral, capital gains tax rate, tax basis protection)
6. Optional dividend for investor (save transaction costs)
7. Firm can buy odd lots of its stock
8. Signal to market (stock is undervalued, etc.)
9. Buy shares for corporate use (avoid dilution)
10. Flexible dividend (for firm and for investors)
11. Best use of cash?
12. Each of the above deserves expansion.

Some generalizations

1. The percentage increase in stock price does not depend on (k-g).
2. The magnitude of D (as log as it is positive) does not affect the percentage increase in stock price.
3. The magnitude of t_p is important!

Conclusions

1. For financial strategies to increase value, the firm must have value.
2. Distribution policy is powerful with many facets.
3. With private equity, the recommended strategies tend to be implemented.

Lecture 20

A Financial Restructuring Strategy

This talk was given in 1993, but I do not know to whom it was given. The talk illustrates one strategy for a corporation to use debt to increase the stockholder's value.

We will compare a financial strategy of keeping the percentage of debt constant with a strategy of immediately issuing \$10,000 million of new debt and repurchasing shares with the debt proceeds. The objective of this financial restructuring is to add shareholder value.

First, we will consider the value in ten years of the stockholders' position without an issue of debt in excess of the amount needed to keep the debt-equity ratio constant.

Secondly, it will be assumed that \$10,000 of debt is issued and an equal amount of stock is purchased. Rather than issue the new debt in the market the current shareholders can be offered an exchange of debt for stock alternative.

No New Debt at Time Zero

This firm does not engage in share repurchase and does not have a dividend reinvestment plan (alternatively, the dollar amount of share repurchase is exactly equal to the amount of dividends reinvested). In addition, it is assumed that:

$$\frac{\text{Debt}}{\text{Stock}} = .445 \quad \frac{\text{Debt}}{\text{Debt} + \text{Stock}} = .31$$

Table 1: Growth = .101, Return on Equity = .12

Year	Dividend (g = .101)	Earnings	Stock Price	P/E
1	$1.200	$3.53	$54.55	15.45
2	1.321	3.887		
3	1.455	4.279		
4	1.602	4.711		
5	1.763	5.187		
6	1.941	5.711		
7	2.137	6.288		
8	2.353	6.923		
9	2.591	7.622		
10	2.853	8.392	$129.68	15.45

Retention rate = .66, r = .12, k_e = .123, t = .36, Initial Dividend = $1.20 per year.

Above, r is the return on new investment, k_e is the cost of equity capital.

After tax interest rate = (1 − .36).073 = .047

$$g = \text{Retention rate}\left[r + \frac{\text{Dept}}{\text{Stock}}(r - \text{AT Interest})\right]$$

$$g = .66[.12 + .445(.12 - .047)] = .101$$

$$P = \frac{1.20}{.123 - .101} = \$54.55.$$ Assume $54.55 is also the market price.

Table 1 shows the dividends and earnings both growing at a rate of .101 for nine years. The stock price grows from $54.55 to $129.68 and the price-earnings multiplier stays constant at 15.45.

$$54.55(1.101)^9 = \$129.68$$

Assume there are 290,800,000 shares outstanding.

V_u (at year 10)	= 290,800,000($129.68)	= $37,711,000,000
V_u (Initial)	= 290,800,000(54.55)	= $15,863,000,000
	Value Increase	$21,848,000,000

Table 2: Total Dividends, Retention, and New Debt (dollar amounts in millions)

Year	Net Income	Total Dividends	Retention	New Debt (.445 of retention)
1	1,029.2	349.0	680.2	303
2	1,133.1	384.2	748.9	333
3	1,247.6	423.1	824.5	367
4	1,373.6	465.8	907.8	404
5	1,512.3	512.8	999.5	445
6	1,665.1	564.6	1,100.5	490
7	1,833.3	621.7	1,211.6	539
8	2,018.4	684.4	1,334.0	594
9	2,222.3	733.6	1,468.7	654
10	2,446.7	829.7	1,617.0	720
			Total New Debt	4,849

The total shareholder value at time 10 is $37,711,000,000 if the growth forecasts are realized. Table 2 shows the total dividends and retention amounts for each year. The model's objective is to keep the two values (retention and cash flows to investors) for each year unchanged with $10,000 million of debt substituted for common equity. Instead of "dividends", with the substitution of debt for equity the equivalent measure of benefits for investors will be "interest plus dividends". Table 2 shows that this model assumes that new debt of $4,849 million will be added (keeping the debt equity rate constant at .445).

Issue Debt and Repurchase Shares

We want the firm with the initial debt issue to be the equivalent of the zero initial debt firm. Therefore, the amount of investment for each year will be kept equal to the amount invested by the first firm. Also, the total cash flow to investors will be kept the same for each year. Any extra resources will be invested into a bond fund earning the same rate as the outstanding .073 bonds (it can be assumed that these .073 bonds are being purchased). The after tax earnings rate on these investments is $.073(1 - .36) = .04672$.

Table 3: Amount Available to Buy Bonds (dollar amounts in millions)

Year	Net Income	After Tax Interest 730(1 − .36) = 467.2	Net Income After Interest	Target Retention	Available to Buy Bonds
1	1,029.2	467.2	562.0	680.2	−118.2
2	1,133.1	467.2	665.9	748.9	−83.0
3	1,247.6	467.2	780.4	824.5	−44.1
4	1,373.6	467.2	906.4	907.8	−1.4
5	1,512.3	467.2	1,045.1	999.5	+45.6
6	1,665.1	467.2	1,197.9	1,100.5	+97.4
7	1,833.3	467.2	1,366.1	1,211.6	+154.5
8	2,018.4	467.2	1,551.2	1,334.0	+217.2
9	2,222.3	467.2	1,755.1	1,468.7	+286.4
10	2,446.7	467.2	1,979.5	1,617.0	+362.5
				PV(.04672) =	$564.5
			Future Value = $(1.04672)^9 564.5$ = $851		

The firm immediately issues $10,000 (million) of .073 debt and buys:

$$\frac{10,000}{54.55} = 183,000,000 \text{ shares of common stock.}$$

After the share repurchase there are:

$$290,800,000 - 183,000,000 = 107,800,000$$

shares outstanding.

Table 3 shows that to meet the target retention amount (keeping investment the same as with zero new initial debt) additional capital is needed in the first four years. Also, the net income increases require that the debt be increased each year consistent with the calculations of Table 2.

Table 3 shows that the firm can invest the same amount as with zero initial new debt and the extra cash generated by operations will total $851 million after ten years.

We still have to consider the position of the investors. The firm pays $730 million of interest each year on the initial debt. Table 4

Table 4: Excess Cash Flow to Investors (dollar amounts in millions)

Year	Paid Interest	Target Dividend*	Excess Cash Flow to Investors
1	730	349.0	381
2	730	384.2	346
3	730	423.1	307
4	730	465.8	264
5	730	512.8	217
6	730	564.6	165
7	730	621.7	108
8	730	684.4	46
9	730	753.6	−24
10	730	829.7	−100

*The dividend of the zero initial new debt firm.

shows that except for years 9 and 10 the $730 million exceeds the dividend on stock the investors would have received without the restructuring.

If we assume the investors can earn an after-tax return of .04672 then the present value of the excess cash flows is $1,497 and the future value is $2,363.

After the ten years the firm needs to retire the $10,000 debt. Assume it issues at a price of $129.68 the 107,800,000 share repurchased at time zero.

$$107,800,000(129.68) = \$13,980,000,000.$$

Retiring the $10,000,000,000 of debt leaves $3,980,000,000 for distribution to the common shareholders. The total net benefits are:

Issuance of stock	$3,980,000,000
Excess benefits to investors	2,363,000,000
Excess investment by firm	851,000,000
Total Benefits	$7,194,000,000

The annual tax savings for ten years are \$262.8. Using the after tax borrowing rate .04672 as the discount rate we have:

$$\text{PV} = 262.8\ \text{B}(10, .04672) = 262.8(7.84622) = 2,061.99$$
$$\text{FV} = (1.04672)^{10} 2,061.99 = \$3,255.$$

There are clear tax savings of \$3,255 million (future value).

Using .123 as the discount rate the tax benefits have a value of \$4,679 million:

$$\text{PV} = 262.8\ \text{B}(10, .123) = 262.8(5.5815) = \$1,466.82$$
$$\text{FV} = (1.123)^{10} 1,466.82 = \$4,679.$$

The total benefits of the restructuring strategy are computed above to be \$7,194,000,000 for ten years. At time 10 the firm is identical to the firm which followed the conventional strategy. Without the restructuring the expected value increase from growth is \$21,848,000,000. With the restructuring, the value increase is:

$$21,848,000,000 + 7,194,000,000 = \$29,042,000,000$$

The increase in value results from two facts:

1. the interest tax shields
2. the use of .073 debt instead of .123 equity for ten years.

The use of the low cost debt is not without risk for the common stockholders.

Also, the total cash flow to investors was maintained, not the cash dividend. Maintaining the cash dividend would result in an increase in the amount of cash to the investors and this would have to be considered. Also, the corporation would have to raise additional debt capital to finance the dividend. A variation would be to use zero coupon debt to conserve cash.

Conclusions

The \$10,000 million amount of debt was arbitrarily chosen to illustrate the consequences of a financial restructuring. A more modest strategy can be implemented with more modest final results. But these more modest results will be consistent with the above example.

Given the fact that it is difficult to make money in this highly competitive world, the proposed strategy has merit. The financial risks are larger, but the operating risks are also large. A profitable firm should consider a financial strategy that adds to risk, but also adds significantly to expected return.

Lecture 21

Ten Suggestions (1995)

I do not remember the location of this talk.

Ten Suggestions for the MBA Class of 1995

1. Spend time with your family. Keep in mind the primary goals of your life. Where do you want to be 40 years from now? What is really important?
2. Take care of your health.
3. Have fun on the job. Either look forward to Monday morning and be enthusiastic on the job or look for another job. Do not take yourself too seriously.
4. The glass is half full! Be optimistic. A cliché, but...!
5. Commit yourself to trying. Try for success. Try to win. Try for excellence, <u>but do something</u>. Take thoughtful risks.
6. Do not be bitter about the way life or the job has treated you. Rejections are the stepping stones to success. Don't look back with regret. Ration your complaints. If things are not going well, look at yourself. See if the thing that is going badly is partially your fault. "The fault, Dear Brutus, is not in our stars but in ourselves, that we are underlings."
7. If you cannot change it, forget it. If there are no alternatives, you don't have a decision.
8. Be honest. Have a conscience. Remember life is a double entry system.

9. Be nice. Treat others as you would have them treat you. Say "thank you" when appropriate. Give credit. Be considerate. Be ethical. As a worldly philosopher once said, "To lose is bad, to lose badly is worse."
10. Listen to the people around you. There will be bright people in your organization. Listen to them. Learn from them.

"In order to get something done, the first step is to get out of bed in the morning." (Bill Strong's grandfather).

One final thought. Many people cannot see beyond their self-interest to see their self-interest.

Lecture 22

Financial Strategies for Value Enhancement

A lecture given sometime in 1990–2000 in the United States.

How Does One Increase the Value of a Firm Through Finance?

<u>Consider:</u>
a. Capital Budgeting
b. Capital Structure
c. Dividend Policy
d. Other

a. Capital Budgeting

a. The choice of the discount rate(s).
b. Valuing real options.
c. Buy versus lease decisions.
d. Performance measurement consistent with good investment policies.
e. Risk Management

b. Capital Structure

With no costs of financial distress it can be shown that:

$$\mathrm{V_L = V_u + tB}$$

where

V_L is the value of the levered firm
V_u is the value of the unlevered firm
t is the corporate tax rate
B is the debt that is added in substitution of common stock equity.

With maximum dept and t = .35 we have

$$V_L = \frac{V_u}{1 - t} = 1.54\, V_u$$

If t = .35, value can be increased by 54%.

But there are complexities:

a. Investor taxes.
b. Costs of financial distress (including an inability of the firm to execute real plans).
c. Stockholders benefit, but CEO incurs the cost. Today there is little or no incentive for a firm to increase the percentage of debt.
d. Consider the growth of private equity.

c. Dividend versus Retained Earnings

Investor earns .064 (tax rate is .36).

Corporation earns .10.

A fifteen year horizon.

With a \$100 dividend and then investment for 15 years.

$$(1 - .36)100(1.064)^{15} = \$162$$

With retention:

$$100(1.10)^{15} = \$418$$

With retention and then a capital gains taxed at .15:

$$100(1.10)^{15}(1 - .15) = \$355$$

Value is more than doubled by retention. Also, there are the savings of the other fourteen years.

Dividend or Share Repurchase?

Consider a share repurchase. The cash flow to investors is \$100 but this is taxed ($t_g = .15$).

With more than \$100 of tax basis, the investor nets more than \$100.

With \$100 of tax basis, the investor nets \$100.

With \$0 of tax basis, the investor nets .85(100) = \$85, but may not sell.

With dividends ($t_d = .15$), the investor nets \$85.

Share Repurchase: Stock Price Effect

Stock Price Effect (Initial Price = \$20: 100,000 shares)

Common Stock Value	\$2,000,000
less (repurchase)	−200,000
New Value	\$1,800,000

After dividend of \$200,000:

$$P = \frac{1{,}800{,}000}{100{,}000} = \$18$$

After share repurchase (10,000 shares)

$$P = \frac{1{,}800{,}000}{90{,}000} = \$20 \text{(no change from \$20)}$$

But through time with Div equal to 10% of market capitalization the price will grow at:

$$g = \frac{\text{Div}}{\text{V} - \text{Div}} = \frac{200{,}000}{2{,}000{,}000 - 200{,}000} = 0.111$$

Assumes zero real growth.

$$P_1 = \frac{2{,}000{,}000}{90{,}000} = \$22.22$$

At time 10, the stock price can be expected to be:

$$P_{10} = 20(1.111)^{10} = \$57.30$$

Share Repurchase

1. Stock price effect
2. EPS effect (and other cosmetic changes)
3. Firm buys undervalued stock
4. Partial LBO
5. Tax effects for investor (tax deferral, capital gains tax rate, tax basis protection)
6. Optional dividend for investor (save transaction costs)
7. Firm can buy odd lots of its stock
8. Signal to market (stock is undervalued etc.)
9. Buy shares for corporate use (avoid dilution)
10. Flexible dividend (for firm and for investors)
11. Best use of cash?
12. Each of the above deserves expansion

Conclusions

1. For financial strategies to increase value, the firm must have value.
2. Capital structure and distribution policy are powerful with many facets.
3. With private equity, the recommended capital structure and dividend strategies tend to be implemented.

Lecture 23

Corporate Finance: A Brief History

The date and the occasion of the talk are not known. If I had known that I was going to assemble this book, I would have kept a better record. There is a lesson here.

Corporate Finance: The Past, Present, and the Future

It is an honor and a pleasure to be addressing the faculty, friends, and alumni of our schools on this significant occasion.

This evening I will talk to you about the changes in corporate finance that have occurred in the past 40 years and some changes likely to occur in the future. This format allows me to suggest some changes that I think should occur. But to put all logical financial decision techniques in perspective consider the words of the late world famous historian Carl Becker in describing how Ezra Cornell made the fortune that enabled him and Andrew Dickson White to found Cornell University.[1] "Ezra Cornell acquired a fortune, as one may say, by misadventure, by violating all the rules of prudence and common sense and adhering, with stubborn tenacity, contrary to experience and all sound advice, to a settled conviction". The conviction was that the telegraph business would be a success. But his actual success story is complex and difficult to evaluate. Cornell was an economic failure, deeply in debt, until competitive telegraph

---

[1]Carl L. Becker, Cornell University, Founders and the Founding Cornell University Press, Ithaca, 1943, p. 52.

firms convinced Cornell to sell his firm and help form the monopoly "Western Union Telegraph Company". Cornell became a millionaire. There are lessons in this story that I do not want you to learn. But more "joint ventures" and expanded "cooperation" are two forecasts for the future.

Now we will briefly review the history of the academic discipline of corporate finance as well as the contributions of corporate finance practice.

Corporate finance received a major thrust 43 years ago. In 1951 two books were published that opened the door to new managerial techniques for making capital budgeting decisions using discounted cash flow methods of evaluating investments. *Capital Budgeting* was written by Joel Dean and *The Theory of Investment of the Firm* by Vera and Friedrich Lutz.

Dean, a respected academician who did a large amount of business consulting, wrote his book for business teachers and managers. The Lutzes were economists interested in capital theory, and wrote their book for the economic academic community. Both books were extremely well written and are understandable. They initially caused academics and subsequently business managers to rethink how investments should be reevaluated. Up to the late 1950's payback and accounting return on investment were the two primary capital budgeting methods used by large firms, with less than 5% of the largest firms using a DCF method.

Today, almost all large corporations use at least one DCF method. Unfortunately, approximately 50% of these firms also still use accounting ROI to evaluate investments. This is unfortunate since ROI is a very flawed technique for evaluating investments.

The second major thrust in corporate finance came in June 1958 when Franco Modigliani and Merton Miller published their classic paper on capital structure in the *American Economic Review.*

The paper proved that the value of a firm was independent of its capital structure, thus the firm's capital structure decision was irrelevant. Fortunately, this faulty conclusion was soon adjusted to the correct position that in the presence of corporate income taxes and financial distress costs, capital structure would affect value. The position was then adjusted to consider the effect of investor taxes on the capital structure decision. Today, there is agreement that capital structure decisions are important, though a clever tax law can decrease their importance.

In 1964, William Sharpe, building on Harry Markowitz's portfolio theory, derived the Capital Asset Pricing Model (CAPM). This model which directly affects investment strategy also greatly affects corporate finance. It suggests that unsystematic risk is diversified away by investors thus not relevant, but that systematic risk must be considered. Firms do not have to diversify activities to reduce risk, investors can diversify to the extent they desire diversification.

In 1973 there was the fourth major development. Fischer Black and Myron Scholes published a paper in *The Journal of Political Economy* on the pricing of options, and offered a unique method of valuing options. The Black-Scholes valuation formula already widely used by all financial markets is about to be the basis of valuing options given to managers for purposes of measuring accounting income in the U.S. It is also highly important for many hedging activities and has significant capital budgeting implications that are beginning to be understood. Most importantly, option theory introduces a new way to think about corporate finance.

In the 1980s, academic theory development took second place to three real world financial developments. One was the development of the junk bond market and the tremendous implications this market had to corporate finance practices. The second development was the initiation of the swap market and its rapid growth. The third development was the rapid expansion in the market for futures and derivative securities. The origin of important corporate financial developments is not restricted to the academic community.

But now let us switch to the more challenging part of my talk. Where is corporate finance today and where is it heading?

Let us return to the topic of capital budgeting where today 100% Or nearly 100% of the largest industrial firms use one or more DCF methods. The first and easiest step for improvement is for firms to stop using the ROI method for evaluating investments. This method is misleading and supplies no useful information.

The second improvement is more difficult, but also more important. It is not likely to be correct to apply the formula $(1+\mathrm{r})^{-\mathrm{n}}$ using one value of r to transform all cash flows of all time periods back to the present, if r includes both a pure time value and a risk factor. Thus I forecast better methods of taking into consideration risk and time value than using a risk adjusted discount rate (r) in the formula $(1+\mathrm{r})^{-\mathrm{n}}$.

Consider a situation where a \$1,000 contractual cash flow to be received at time 1 has .9 probability of being received (the expected value is \$900) and risk aversion reduces the expected value to a certainty equivalent of .8(900) = \$720. With a .10 risk free discount rate the present value of the certainty equivalent is:

$$\mathrm{PV} = \frac{720}{1.10} = \$654.55$$

This is equivalent to discounting the time 1 \$900 expected value by .375

$$\mathrm{PV} = \frac{900}{1.375} = \$654.54$$

Now assume the same payoff takes place at time 10 so that the present value of the certainty equivalent is now:

$$\mathrm{PV} = \frac{720}{(1.10)^{10}} = \$277.59$$

This is equivalent to discounting the \$900 expected value by .12482.

$$\mathrm{PV} = \frac{900}{(1.12482)^{10}} = \$277.59$$

When the cash flow occurred at time one, .375 was the equivalent risk adjusted rate. When the cash flow occurred at time 10, .12482 was the equivalent risk adjusted rate. The risk adjusted discount rate is different for each cash flow received in a different time period. For many long-lived investments a lower discount rate should be used for cash flows that are more distant in time.

We also need to reconsider the capital structure choice. One has to be careful here since the recommendation has to be location specific. In the United States, with Drexel Burnham driven out of existence, firms no longer have an incentive to design a shareholder value maximizing capital structure. The pressure from raiders is off. Raiders find it difficult to raise capital.

Let us take a closer look at Drexel-Burnham and junk bonds. It is important to understand what junk bonds (and Drexel Burnham) did and did not do.

They did:

a. finance the acquisition of real assets
b. finance acquisitions of firms
c. finance LBOs
d. reduce the income taxes of some restructured firms and increase shareholder value
e. cause uneasiness in many board rooms
f. give investors an interesting choice (high risk high yield debt).

They did not:

a. increase the risk of any issuing corporation (they did increase the risk of the remaining stock)
b. they did not increase the risk to investors (initial equity investors could subsequently increase or decrease their risk)
c. they did not put economically desirable workers out of jobs (economically profitable workers were retained by profit minded investors).
d. they did not decrease social welfare.

Junk bonds are a means of financing, more risky than investment grade debt, but less risky than an equal amount of equity for the same corporation. They deserve careful analysis, not a negative evaluation based on prejudice and emotion.

Have there been junk bond defaults? Yes, there have been and they were predictable (not the specific defaults, but the fact there would be defaults). Assume that on issue junk bonds yielded 800 basis points above the Government's default free rate (r), this implies that if r = .08, that the probability of debt payment was approximately:

$$p = \frac{1+r}{1+k} = \frac{1.08}{1.16} = .93$$

and the probability of default in each year was $1 - p = .07$. For a ten year period the probability of default at some time for the bond was .52! The market demanded a substantive risk premium for junk bonds because the market knew there would be defaults. The market works a great deal better than business news-reporters are willing to admit.

A redesign of the capital structure of the average U.S. firm could increase stockholder value by 40 to 50%. A change in dividend policy could add another 30 to 40% in value.

Assume a corporate tax rate of .35, and the relationship

$$V_L = V_u + tB$$

applies where

V_L is the value of the levered firm
V_u is the value of the unlevered firm
t is the corporate tax rate
B is the debt issued in substitution for common stock.

If maximum debt is issued so that $B = V_L$ and all the tax deductions can be used, then

$$V_L = V_u + tV_L$$

and

$$V_L = \frac{V_u}{1-t}$$

With t = .35, then

$$V_L = 1.54\ V_u$$

The fully levered firm has 54% more value than the unlevered firm.

When in the U.S. the top tax rate on ordinary income was 28% and the capital gains rate was 28% George Bush wanted to decrease the tax on capital gains. He failed. But Bill Clinton, by raising the top tax rate on ordinary income to 39.6% or higher has effectively reduced the tax on capital gains. The tax on ordinary income is now $\frac{.396}{.28} - 1 = .41$ larger than the tax on capital gains.

Assume a company is earning \$1 and paying a \$1 dividend. The tax is .396 and investors discount the dividend using 10. The value is:

$$\text{PV} = \frac{1(1 - .396)}{.10} = \$6.04$$

If instead of a dividend the company repurchases shares, the investors are taxed at a .28 rate (the worst case has a zero tax basis for the investment) and the value is now:

$$\text{PV} = \frac{1(1 - .028)}{.10} = \$7.20$$

This is an improvement in value of 19.2%.

In addition, significant gains can be obtained by a tax deferral strategy. For example, if the corporation earns a return of .1656 after corporate tax, then if \$1 is retained for 10 years and then the investor has a capital gains tax, the investor has

$$1(1.1656)^{10}(1 - .28) = \$3.33$$

compared to a dividend that is taxed and reinvested to earn .10 (after investor tax):

$$1(1 - .396)(1.10)^{10} = \$1.57$$

The tax deferral combined with a change to a capital gains tax results in more than a doubling of value.

I predict that some investors seeking increased returns will discover that corporate financial engineering can double the shareholders' value and that there will be moves to exploit these opportunities.

Ultimately, I forecast that governments will become aware that all capital sources are equivalent (back to M M, 1958) and should be taxed on an equivalent (equal handed) manner. It might take longer for the U.S. Government to take action, but someday, even a U.S. corporation will not be able to find a tax advantage in financial engineering. That is not the situation today. There is money to be made.

My third area of forecast is easy. It is already happening. I would have forecasted that firms that had diversified beyond their expertise to reduce risk would reverse the process. The banks and investment banks that earned fees on the acquisition would earn fees on the divestments. This all is occurring and will continue to occur.

My fourth forecast has to do with the growth of the derivative market associated with hedging operations. My first forecast in this area is that firms will switch from each operating unit doing its own hedging to hedging from a corporate world-wide perspective. Secondly, I forecast that firms will reconsider the cost-benefits of hedging. Who benefits from costly hedging operations? I am not forecasting the disappearance of hedging, but rather more of a willingness to accept a reasonable level of risk. We all have life insurance when we have small children and we tend to insure our homes against fire and other disasters. But there are other risks of loss that we are willing to accept and do not insure. In like manner, corporations do not need to hedge all hedgeable risks.

My fifth forecast has to do with corporate ownership. I expect shareholders to increase their activity in controlling the activities of business. This applies to institutional investors, but also to a second group of shareholders. We will see more corporations controlled by their managers and workers through stock ownership.

In the future we can expect there to be relatively more significant changes in financial strategy than changes in financial securities. In the past 20 years innovations in financial securities have been driven by:

a. tax considerations
b. governmental regulations

c. advent of powerful and accessible computers
d. increase in foreign trade and international finance transactions
e. increase in the knowledge of persons working in finance
f. access to computers.

Even if we do not expect the influence of taxation, regulation, computers, and the knowledge of participants to grow significantly, there is reason to expect that there will be a large number of significant security innovations linked to an increase in the volume of foreign currency transactions. The opportunities for improved financial strategies and the opportunities for financial innovations remain large.

The next forecast is a switch from the previous topics. It deals with measuring the performance of managers using financial measures. There is a need to change from using income and ROI as the primary methods to using economic income. We cannot expect managers to make decisions to increase shareholder value if the successful execution of the decisions is to reduce the well-being of the managers. There must be congruence between the objectives of the firm and the ways in which managerial performance is measured.

Assume a \$100,000,000 division is earning a .30 ROI for a company with a .09 cost of capital. The manager receives praise and a large bonus. But assume a \$200,000,000 investment opportunity that would earn .20 is rejected because it would lower the division's ROI. This sequence is not desirable from the stockholders' viewpoint.

An improved system would report $30{,}000{,}000 - 9{,}000{,}000 =$ \$21,000,000 of economic income without the investment and

$$21{,}000{,}000 + 40{,}000{,}000 - 18{,}000{,}000 = \$43{,}000{,}000$$

of economic income with the investment.

Any desirable investment will enhance the economic income measure (either over the life of the asset or with economic depreciation in every year of the asset's life).

There is one final forecast, which is the most important and the safest of all forecasts. Future events will be different than those forecasted by me or by anyone else. The only way to cope with the future is to have a fundamental understanding of good corporate decision-making and analyze using good theory the new economic environment when it arrives.

Future corporate finance experts will be concerned with the same types of problems as we are. There will never be a capital budgeting method that insures that the cash flow imputs are perfectly correct. There will never be a capital structure model that allows us to perfectly balance the tax and other advantages of one capital structure with the costs of financial distress. There are few, if any, perfect financial hedges.

I offer to you one final thought, written by Thomas Macauley and contained in his "History of England" — "Those who compare the age on which their lot has fallen with a golden age which exists only in their imagination may talk of degeneracy and decay: but no man who is correctly informed as to the past will be disposed to take a morose or desponding view of the present."

These are the best of times, except for those of the future, and together we can improve the future.

Lecture 24

Graduation 1980

This graduation address was prepared but was not given. Life has its disappointments.

Last year I gave my best lecture at graduation. When asked to talk again this year, my original impulse was to give my second best lecture. But this class was much too good to settle for second best, so I consulted with BCG and decided that I had the equivalent of a cash cow and I should milk it. So you are about to hear last year's graduation address, revised so that not even last year's class would recognize it.

One warning to those who intend not to listen until the second half of the address. There is no second half.

Last year I gave ten suggestions for success and revealed the ten most important things that you learned at BPA. This year I am going to concentrate on the former.

My ten somewhat plagiarized advices for a manager are:

1. Don't neglect your family. Keep in mind the real objective of your life. Where do you want to be 40 years from now?
2. Take care of your health. Even I jog.
3. Have fun on the job. Either look forward to Monday morning and be enthusiastic or look for another job.
4. The glass is half full! Be optimistic.
5. Commit yourself to trying. Give it your best shot. Try for excellence. Try for success.

6. Give up the right to be bitter. "Rejections are the stepping stones to success." Don't look back with regret. Don't always complain. Ration your complaints. If things are not going well, look at yourself. See if the thing that is wrong is partially your fault.
7. If you cannot change it, forget it. If there are no alternatives, you don't have a decision.
8. Be honest. Have a conscience. Remember life is a double entry system.
9. Be nice. Treat others as you would have them treat you. Say "thank you" when appropriate. Give credit. Be nicely competitive. Play the game. As a worldly philosopher once said, "To lose is bad, to lose badly is worse."
10. Read my next book. Especially the rhymes.

For years I have been giving out wisdoms. My wife calls it "pontificating." Sometime in the midst of the past winter I made a discovery. Some guy by the name of Ralph Waldo Emerson had plagiarized my best observations.

To extract from Emerson's writings without leaving behind important words is impossible. I have extracted, but I apologize for having done it.

On Self-Reliance

"A man should learn to detect and watch that gleam of light which flashes across his mind from within, more than the lustre of the firmament of bards and sages. Yet he dismisses without notice his thought, because it is his. In every work of genius we recognize our own rejected thoughts: they come back to us with a certain alienated majesty. Great works of art have no more affecting lesson for us than this. They teach us to abide by our spontaneous impression with good humored inflexibility then most when the whole cry of voices is on the other side. Else, tomorrow a stranger will say with masterly good sense precisely what we have thought and felt all the time, and we shall be forced to take with shame our own opinion from another."

"A foolish consistency is the hobgoblin of little minds, adored by little statesmen and philosophers and divines." With consistency a great soul has simply nothing to do."

On Compensation

"An inevitable dualism bisects nature, so that each thing is a half, and suggests another thing to make it whole; as spirit, matter; man, woman; subjective, objective; in, out; upper, under; motion, rest; yea, nay.

While the world is thus dual, so is every one of its parts. The entire system of things gets represented in every particle. There is somewhat that resembles the ebb and flow of the sea, day and night, man and woman, in a single needle of the pine, in a kernel of corn, in each individual of every animal tribe."

"The farmer imagines power and place are fine things. But the President has paid dear for his White House. It has commonly cost him all his peace and the best of his manly attributes. To preserve for a short time so conspicuous an appearance before the world, he is content to eat dust before the real masters who stand erect behind the throne."

"The dice of God are always loaded. The world looks like a multiplication table or a mathematical equation, which, turn it how you will, balances itself. Take what figure you will, its exact value, no more nor less, still returns to you. Every secret is told, every crime is punished, every virtue rewarded, every wrong redressed, in silence and certainty."

The next two quotes are for my business policy course students.

On Power

"All successful men have agreed in one thing, — they were causationists. They believed that things went not by luck, but by law; that there was not a weak or a cracked link in the chain that joins the first and last of things. A belief in causality, or strict connection between every trifle and the principle of being, and, in consequence, belief in compensation, or, that nothing is got for nothing — characterizes all valuable minds and must control every effort that is made by an industrious one."

"Some persons make things happen 'Whatever befalls, befalls him first ...''' And finally the quote for my faculty colleagues:

"Empirical science is apt to cloud the sight, and, by the very knowledge of functions and processes, to bereave the student of the manly contemplation of the whole. The savant becomes unpoetic."

Taking up Emerson's challenge of remaining poetic I have two poems for you. The first a somewhat bitter lament by Oliver Wendell Holmes:

"Don't you know that people won't employ
A man that wrongs his manliness by laughing like a boy?"

The second is by Florence M. Kelso:

"You buy the stock, you own the store."
Free enterprisers laud it.
But no one listens when I say
More dividends, and by the way
Because my son's a C.P.A.
Let's have him do our audit.

One final observation. As you proceed with your career, you will have doubts whether you chose the right job with the right firm. Right, Bob Hennessy? Put those doubts aside; you made the right decision. Now and in the future, the important thing is whether or not you do something with the job, not whether the job is the best job.

Any college teacher is apt to have similar doubts about the job. Is teaching really worth the effort? Associating with the class of 1980 at Cornell's BPA has kept the doubts from my mind for one more year. It has truly been a pleasure knowing you for two years. If you fulfill the promise of your capabilities, you will achieve much. I thank you for a great two years.

Lecture 25

Financial Strategies in Uncertain Times

Increasing the value of a firm via corporate finance. This lecture was given in 2003 in Paris and is based on a previous lecture, also in this book.

How does One Increase the Value of a Firm Through Finance?

a. Capital Budgeting
b. Capital structure
c. Dividend policy
d. Other

Capital Budgeting

a. The choice of the discount rate(s).
b. Valuing real options
c. Buy versus lease decisions
d. Performance measurement consistent with good investment policies
e. Risk Management

Capital Structure

With no costs of financial distress it can be shown that:

$$V_L = V_u + tB$$

where

V_L is the value of the levered firm

V_u is the value of the unlevered firm

t is the corporate tax rate

B is the debt that is added in substitution of common stock equity.

With maximum debt and t = .35 we have

$$V_L = \frac{V_u}{1-t} = 1.54\ V_u$$

Value can be increased by 54%.

But there are complexities:

a. Investor taxes
b. Costs of financial distress (including an inability of the firm to execute real plans).
c. Stockholders benefit, but CEO incurs the cost. Today there is little or no incentive for a firm to increase the percentages of debt.
d. Effect of debt issuance on EPS.

Dividend Versus Retained Earnings

Investor earns .064 (tax rate is .36).
Corporation earns .10
A fifteen year horizon.
With a $100 dividend and then investment for 15 years.

$$(1-.36)100(1.064)^{15} = \$162$$

With retention:

$$100(1.10)^{15} = \$418$$

With retention and then a capital gains taxed at .18:

$$100(1.10)^{15}\ (1 - .18) = \$343$$

Value is more than doubled by retention. Also, there are the savings of the other fourteen years.

Tax "Reform"

Assume dividends are allowed as a deduction by the corporation.

$$t_c = .35, t_p = .36, t_g = .20$$

a. What is better, debt or common stock?
b. What is better, dividends or retained earnings?
c. What is better, dividends or share repurchase?

Dividends as Tax Deduction

Debt or common stock?

	Debt	Common Stock	Retained Earnings
EBIT	$100	$100	$100
Interest or Dividend	100	100	
Corporate Tax	0	0	35
Investor Tax	36	36	—
Net	$64	$64	$65*

*There will be a tax to investor when the stock is sold

Debt is not more desirable than stock.

Dividend or share repurchase?

Consider a share repurchase. There is $35 of corporate tax. The cash flow to investors is $65 but this is taxed ($t_g = .20$).
With more than $65 of tax basis the investor nets more than $65.
With $65 of tax basis the investor nets $65.
With $0 of tax basis the investor nets .8(65) = $52.
Dividends give $64. Inconclusive.

Dividends are Not Taxed (Bush Proposal)

$t_p = .36$ but t_p is reduced to Zero for Dividends
$t_c = .35$

No change in corporate taxes

	Debt	Common Stock (Dividend)	Common Stock (Retention)	Common Stock (Share Repurchase)
EBIT	$100	$100	$100	$100
Corporate Tax	0	35	35	35
Investor Tax	36	0	0	Some Tax
Net	$ 64**	$65	$ 65*	Less than $65

1. Common stock beats debt for taxed investor
2. Dividend is as good as retention
3. Dividend beats share repurchase for taxed investor

*There may be some tax in the future (there is a change in the investor's tax basis).

**Could be $100

Dividend is Taxed

Assume Tax on Dividends is Reduced to .20.
$t_g = .20$.

	Debt	Common Stock (Dividend)	Common Stock (Retention)	Common Stock (Share Repurchase)
EBIT	$100	$100	$100	$100
Corporate Tax	0	35	35	35
Investor Tax	36	13*	0**	0**
Net	$64	$52	$65	$65

*Dividend is $65.

**The tax in the future may be as high as .20(65) = $13. But this amount must be time discounted.

Dividends are almost as good as other common stock alternatives, but still inferior.

Dividends Not Taxed: Happy or Sad?

Happy

1. Stocks in taxable accounts.
2. Gov't bond traders (larger U.S. deficit)
3. Investment banks (corporations must raise capital)
4. Bush

Sad

1. Managers who are thoughtful (lose share repurchase as the "obvious" choice)
2. Small or zero shareholders
3. Finance professors
4. Average U.S. citizen
5. Insurance Companies selling annuities or retirement plans.
6. Banks paying interest.

Rankings for Investors (not a forecast)

Before Bush	If Bush Wins
1. Retained Earnings 2. Share Repurchase 3. a. Dividends b. Dividends & DRP	1. Dividends with DRP 2. Dividends (100%) 3. Retained Earnings (deemed a dividend) 4. Share Repurchase (but still popular with managers).
Conclusions: a. Most corporations should not pay dividends b. Managers and shareholders have same strategy preferences.	Conclusions: a. All corporations should pay 100% of earnings as dividends or a deemed dividend. b. Different preference for Managers

Note: a. Partial repeal of Capital Gains Tax (deemed dividend)
b. A record-keeping mess.

Share Repurchase Versus Dividends

Ordinary income tax rate = .36
Capital gains tax rate = .18
Price = Tax Basis = \$20 per share
\$200,000 available. 100,000 shares
(investor owns 1,000 shares).

Cash Dividends

Investor receives \$2 × 1,000 =	\$2,000
Tax (.36)	−720
	\$1,280

Share Repurchase

Investor sells 100 shares
Investor receives 100 × 20 = \$2,000
(no tax, no taxable gain)

Stock Price Effect

$t_p = .39$ and $k - g = .01$: t_p could be smaller

$$P_0 = \frac{(1 - t_p)D}{k - g} = \frac{(1 - .39)1.639}{.10 - .09} = \frac{1}{.01} = \$100$$

Div yield equals to 1.639%

Change t_p to zero:

$$P_1 = \frac{1.639}{.10 - .09} = \$164$$

or

$$\frac{P_1}{P_o} = \frac{1}{1 - t_p} = 1.64$$

If price is set by zero tax investors ($k - g = .01$)

$P_0 = P_1 = \$164$ No Change

k could change with tax law change.

Stock Price Effect (Initial Price = \$20)

Common Stock Value	\$2,000,000
less (repurchase)	−200,000
New Value	\$1,800,000

After dividend:

$$p = \frac{1,800,000}{100,000} = \$18$$

After share repurchase (10,000 shares)

$$P = \frac{1,800,000}{90,000} = \$20(\text{no change})$$

But through time with Div equal to 10% of market capitalization the price will grow at:

$$g = \frac{\text{Div}}{\text{V} - \text{Div}} = \frac{200,000}{2,000,000 - 200,000} = 0.111$$

Assumes zero real growth.

$$P_1 = \frac{2,000,000}{90,000} = \$22.22$$

At time 10 the stock price can be expected to be: $P_{10} = 20(1.111)^{10} = \$57.30$

Share Repurchase

1. Stock price effect
2. EPS effect (and other cosmetic changes)
3. Firm buys undervalued stock
4. Partial LBO
5. Tax effects for investor (tax deferral, capital gains tax rate, tax basis protection)
6. Optional dividend for investor (save transaction costs)
7. Firm can buy odd lots of its stock
8. Signal to market (stock is undervalued, etc.)
9. Buy shares for corporate use (avoid dilution)

10. Flexible dividend (for firm and for investors)
11. Best use of cash?
12. Each of the above deserves expansion.

Some Generalizations

1. The percentage increase in stock price does not depend on (k − g).
2. The magnitude of D (as long as it is positive) does not affect the percentage increase in stock price.
3. The magnitude of t_p is important!

Conclusions

1. For financial strategies to increase value, the firm must have value.
2. Distribution policy is powerful with many facets.
3. With private equity the recommended strategies tend to be implemented.

Lecture 26

A Visit with Alumni

This talk was in Ithaca in or about the year 2000.

Two dimensions to consider:

a. Interest to audience
b. Intellectual vigor

"Interest" wins.

Topic: Some tips on making investment decisions.

Title: "The Bare Essentials of Investing: Teaching the Horse to Talk"

Diversification

Let n be number of securities

$$\text{Feasible Reduction} = \frac{n-1}{n}$$

n	Feasible Reduction of Risk
10	90%
100	99%

Find "independent" investments.

We shall spell "DAMET".[1]

Alternative Investments

Stocks
Bonds (municipal, government, etc.)
Real Estate
TIPs
Private Equity (Blackstone, Fortress, etc.)
Special Taxed Vehicles
Real Assets (exotic)

Market Turns

Can you determine when stock market is too high and you should sell?

Must also determine when the market is low enough to buy.

Efficient Market

Evaluate: "I sell when the stock reaches $40 and buy when the stock falls to $35." — A Learned Professor

Simple decision rules are likely to be too simple.
The market is relatively efficient.

Taxes

The investment choices must take taxes into account. Implications:

a. Stocks should be held in taxable accounts (as long as $t_d = .15$ and $t_g = .15$ and $t_P = .35$).

[1] D for Diversification
A for Analysis or Allocation
M for Market Turns (cannot predict)
E for Efficient Markets (do not go in and out)
T for Tax considerations

b. Debt held in tax deferred accounts.
c. Compare dividends and share repurchase corporate strategies.

Teaching the Horse to Talk

A King has sentenced a teacher to die. To avoid the sentence, the teacher has promised to teach the King's favorite horse to talk.

A friend of the teacher said to the teacher, "Why did you make such a rash promise? You know no one has ever taught a horse to talk." The teacher said in reply, "Sometime before the end of five years:

- The King might change his mind and pardon me.
- The King might forget that he sentenced me to death.
- The King might die. I might die.
- I might teach the horse to talk.

In any event, I gain five years."

Note he did not promise to teach the horse to talk by next week. Why do I claim to know that the stock market is not too high from a long-term perspective? In order to prove that the market is too high from a long-term perspective you are going to need the earnings on stock over the next five, ten, twenty, or more years. The financial history of the U.S. shows that common stocks have been a good long-term investment over the past ninety years. Of course, this does not prove they will be a good investment (compared to alternatives) in the future. That is why diversification is recommended. Ninety years from now you might show stocks have not been a good investment. We shall see.

Suggested Reading: *The Bare Essentials of Investing: Teaching the Horse to Talk* (World Scientific Publishing Co., 2007). Author: Harold Bierman, Jr.

Lecture 27

Economic Forecasting

This lecture was given in the U.S. somewhere between 1990–2000.

We would all like to know the economic future.

We must distinguish between the following.

Things forecastable: Demographics

Things not forecastable:

a. The change in interest rates.
b. The change in real estate prices.
c. Stock market turns.

The stock market crash of 1929 preceded the 1930's depression. Since then, it is said that the stock market has successfully predicted fifteen of the last five recessions.

Exploiting Long Range Forecasting

Long ago in a mid-European country a famous teacher was in trouble with his King. The King sentenced the teacher to death.

The teacher pleaded "Give me five years in which to teach your horse to talk".

The King liked to own unusual things, and after considerable thought said "Yes".

A friend of the teacher said to the teacher "Why did you make such a rash promise? You know no one has ever taught a horse to talk". The teacher said in reply, "Sometime before the end of five years:

1. the King might change his mind.
2. the King might forget.
3. the King might die. I might die.
4. I might teach the horse to talk.

In any event, I gain five years."

Note that he did not promise to teach the horse to talk by the following week.

In 1987, a book was published, *The Great Depression of 1990*, by Ravi Batra of SMU. It sold 400,000 copies in 1987. Batra realized that by the end of 1990:

a. There would be a depression in 1990 and Batra would be a footnote in Economic History and write another book and would be a millionaire.
b. There would not be a depression in 1990 and Batra would be a millionaire.

Forecasting

One thing is certain:

There will be surprises.

You must have contingency plans.

There will be some things we can predict:

a. cheap labor of the Far East and Eastern Europe
b. also large markets of the above
c. an invention or environmental change will depress the value of a large amount of real estate holdings

d. a new management style or technique will sweep the country or at least the business schools

Required: Flexibility and Contingency Plans

Forecasting and You Today

The best year to buy common stock was ________.

Lecture 28

Management of Risk and Capital Budgeting

This is one of only a few talks that were fully written out. The talk was given in 1992 at the Johnson School.

After the management of a firm has completed its planning process, the resulting long range strategic plan has to be translated into a specific plan of action which actually allocates resources. I will call the specific plan to allocate resources the capital budget and capital budgeting is the process of arriving at the plan.

It is convenient to divide investments into two general classifications. First we classify all investment opportunities that are economically independent of each other. Thus an automobile manufacturer might consider replacing its automobile production line with a more labor efficient set of machines, or it might consider entering the airline industry. These are two independent investment alternatives. They compete for financial resources, but their cash flows are economically independent.

Once we have determined the independent investments we must next consider all investments which perform the same economic function, where only one investment will be accepted. These are "mutually exclusive" investments.

The objective of the capital budgeting process is to make accept or reject decisions involving independent investments (we can undertake all independent investments that are desirable) and "best of the set" decisions involving mutually exclusive investments (we can undertake only one of the mutually exclusive investments). In making these investment decisions there is implied some known and agreed upon objective for the firm.

As a first step we should clearly indicate the corporate objectives that are not affecting the capital budgeting process. We are not attempting to maximize total sales or percentage share of market. Growth is not the goal (though growth might occur if the correct decisions are made) nor are earnings per share and total earnings being maximized. The goal is to maximize the risk adjusted net present value of the stockholders' position and we assume that in doing so we are maximizing the well-being of the stockholders. The decisions are being made from the point of view of the stockholders and it is assumed that their interests are best served by a procedure that systematically assigns a cost to the capital that is utilized in the production process.

The capital budgeting process that is recommended must take into consideration a cost on the capital that is being utilized or more generally we can say that the process must take into consideration the time value of money. In addition, the process must also cope with the existence of uncertainty and adjust the analysis for the risk of the project being considered.

Capital budgeting decisions generally involve immediate (or nearly immediate) outlays and benefits that stretch out through time. In some cases the benefits may be deferred for many years. The primary problem facing management responsible for making capital budgeting decisions is to incorporate time value and risk considerations in such a manner that the well-being of the stockholders is maximized. There are no known simple and exact solutions to this problem.

Decision Pitfalls

There are several different types of pitfalls associated with capital budgeting decision procedures. For example, a firm can use an incorrect calculation method. Secondly, the firm can use a correct calculation method, but can use it incorrectly. Third, a firm can have a correct method of evaluating investments, but can evaluate managerial performance incorrectly, and this affects investment decisions. To illustrate the above, consider the following three relevant questions:

a. Does your firm use ROI (with other measures) to evaluate investments?
b. Does your firm use *one* "hurdle rate" or "required return"?
c. Is a division that earns .25 ROI in a year doing better than a division that earns .15? Assume the firm has a .10 cost of money.

"Yes" answers to questions a, b, or c are not acceptable. Let us first consider question a.

If the ROI calculation is based on conventional accounting, it cannot be used effectively to evaluate investments. The ROI measures used to evaluate investments are apt to be misleading since they leave out the time value of money effects.

Consider thc following two investments:

	Cash Flows at Time:		
	0	1	2
Investment A	–10,000	1,000	11,000
Investment B	–10,000	11,000	1,000

A casual inspection of the above reveals that the second investment is to be preferred to the first (the total amount received is the same for both investments, but the second investment receives some cash earlier than the first). The ROI method of evaluating investments will fail to reveal the superiority of B compared to A. For example, the total income over the life of either investment is $2,000 and the average income is $1,000 for an average investment of $5,000. This is a 20% return on investment (ROI) and both investments have this return. The ROI measure does not detect the superiority of B. Alternative ROI measures (e.g. using the ROI's of each year) would also fail to indicate the superiority of B compared to A. ROI as conventionally computed should not be used to evaluate investments.

ROI is an incorrect investment calculation method(flawed from a theoretical viewpoint).

The problem with using one hurdle rate or required return to take into consideration both the time value of money and risk is that each investment alternative is likely to have different risks in different time periods. Using one required return is likely to lead to the rejection of good (safe) investments and the acceptance of bad (risky) investments. While net present value (NPV) is a theoretically correct calculation method, if the discount rate being used is not an accurate representation of the cost of money, the results of the calculations may not be reliable. NPV would be a correct method being used incorrectly.

When is a lower ROI more desirable than a higher ROI? Assume the following facts apply.

	.15 Division	.25 Division
Capital Assets	$2,000,000,000	$500,000,000
Income	300,000,000	125,000,000
ROI	.15	.25

But consider:

	.15 Division	.25 Division
Income	$300,000,000	$125,000,000
Less:		
Interest Cost (.10)	200,000,000	50,000,000
Net Economic Income	$100,000,000	$75,000,000

The .15 division is contributing more "income" and is doing better for the firm than the .25 division. A firm that uses ROI to measure performance has introduced the likelihood that desirable investments will be rejected so that the firm's (or division's) performance will be enhanced. A firm can have a correct method of evaluating investments, but if ROI (or the equivalent) is used to measure managerial performance, this can adversely affect the quality of the decisions being made.

Capital Budgeting

Among the things we know about capital budgeting are:

a. NPV and IRR can both be used to evaluate correctly independent investments. The present value profile is a very useful method of presenting alternatives.
b. Mutually exclusive investment decisions are easily solved using NPV and may be solved equally correctly, but with more difficulty using IRR.
c. Payback (used with care) supplies some information concerning risk, but should not be the primary method used.
d. ROI (do not use). A stockholder should pay money to keep this measure of investment desirability off the decision maker's desk.

But consider the following from a Fortune 500 top manager:[1]

> We use several different financial measures in evaluating investment proposals including Internal Rate of Return (IRR), Discounted Payback, Profitability Index, and "Proof Year" Operating Return on Investment.

Note the use of ROI and the exclusion of NPV. This is troublesome. ROI is used extensively (as a secondary method of evaluation) by major industrial firms to evaluate investments. This is a major deficiency in the quality of investment decision making.

The two issues for which there are not easily applied accepted solutions are:

a. Capital rationing which is caused by:

   Scarce resources (e.g. engineering talent)
   Scarce money (solutions are a programming problem or "beauty" contest)

The scarce resource problem may be easily solved by adjusting the input cost measure for the resource. The scarce money situation can theoretically be solved by a programming solution, but the

---

[1]The quotations are from H. Bierman, *Implementation of Capital Budgeting Techniques*, Financial Management Association, Tampa, Florida, 1986.

information requirements are immense, and the information is not likely to be readily available to management Ad hoc solutions using IRR or the index of profitability are not reliable. Judgment (or a beauty contest) is not a bad alternative method of solution. Investments would still have to satisfy the NPV or IRR criteria.

The remainder of the talk will deal with capital budgeting under uncertainty.

b. Uncertainty-Risk

When we consider the uncertainty problem, the need for exact solutions for capital rationing situations is greatly reduced, since the underlying uncertainties are so important.

Uncertainty

The largest number of business decisions are made under conditions of uncertainty. Unfortunately, there are no easy answers or simple formulas that can be applied with exactness when the outcomes are uncertain. We will define uncertainty to exist when more than one outcome is possible. The uncertainty becomes burdensome when one or more of the possible outcomes are undesirable. We call this risk. If we can win either $1,000,000 or $2,000,000 there is uncertainty. If we can either win $1,000,000 or lose $50,000 there is risk.

A primary problem that complicates the analysis is that the relative importance of the time value adjustment and the risk adjustment will vary among investments that have the same type of risk but with the cash flows occurring in different time periods. The implication of this is that the use of one risk adjusted discount rate to evaluate all investments, or even to evaluate all the cash flows of one investment is likely to give misleading results.

The practical problems of capital budgeting under uncertainty are highlighted by the following statement by a Fortune 100 manager:

> In addition to organizational complexity, we are faced with capital budgeting lead times for new technology capacity that often exceed the horizon of our strategic planning process for individual products.

> Occasionally, we are investing in capacity to house machinery and equipment that has not been invented that will produce products not yet on the drawing boards of the product development divisions. Clearly, the uncertainties and risks of this environment make analytical analysis of capital budgeting an art at best.

Rather than one solution, I propose the following methods of coping with uncertainty:

1. Payback and WACC
2. Risk adjusted discount rates
3. Simulation
   (listing outcomes)
   Monte Carlo
4. Sensitivity analysis
   (change the value of the variables)
5. Utility analysis
6. CAPM
7. Option Theory
8. A Simplified Discounting Rule

1. *Payback and WACC*

What payback period is required? Should the required payback period depend on the life of the investment or the timing of the cash flows? Payback can be used to give an impression of risk or safety, but it cannot be used as a general measure of profitability.

The weighted average cost of capital (WACC) is an average return that is a reasonable overall target for the firm but tells us little about whether a specific investment should be undertaken.

Note the word average in "Weighted Average Cost of Capital". Can you apply an average cost of capital to an unique investment? It is likely that the WACC should not be applied to the specific investment whose value is being calculated because the risk (or cash flow) characteristics are not average.

2. *Risk Adjusted Discount Rates*

The most widely used method is the risk adjusted discount rate. If a safe investment must earn .10, a risky investment must be expected to earn more. The procedure is easy to implement, but it is very difficult to analyze exactly what is being accomplished. Does risk increase exponentially through time? This is implied by the use of $(1+j)^{-n}$ where j is a risk adjusted discount rate. The mix of time and risk leading to one discount rate used for investments with different lives is not a reliable process.

Consider the following example. With a .07 discount rate the firm needs \$224.23 at time 80 to have \$1 of present value. How many \$ do you need, at time 80, r = .25, to have \$1 of present value?

	Future Values		
r/n	1	20	80
.07	1.07	3.87	224.23
.15	1.15		
.25	1.25		?

The answer to the question is $\$1(1.25)^{80} = \$56,597,994$. The present value of \$56,597,994 received at time 80 is \$1 if the appropriate discount rate is .25. Conclusion: The combination of time value and risk in one calculation is not a reliable process. If the .25 interest rate represents the borrowing rate for the firm, then \$56,597,994 is too low an estimate of the cash flows needed. If the firm's borrowing rate is .08 and there is a .17 risk adjustment for planting safe trees then probably \$56,597,994 is too large. The amount needed for a safe investment is only $\$1(1.08)^{80} = \$772$.

Under what circumstances can we assume that the use of $(1+r)^{-n}$ is correct even if r includes a risk premium? The risk discount (difference between the expected value and certainty equivalent) has to be changing through time.

Certainty equivalents are very attractive in that they are easy to work with, and it might appear that we know what we are doing. But we do not know how to obtain systematically certainty equivalents.

We want to relate certainty equivalents and risk adjusted discount rates.

Let:

CE be the certainty equivalent of the cash flow X

$\bar{X}$ be the expected cash flow

k_o be the risk adjusted discount rate

r_f be the risk free rate

j be the certainty equivalent conversion factor:

$$1 + j = \frac{\bar{X}}{CE}$$

The present value of a cash flow with a certainty equivalent of CE occurring at time n is:

$$PV = (1 + r_f)^{-n} CE$$

If the expected value and the risk adjusted discount rate is used, the present value is:

$$PV = (1 + k_0)^{-n} \bar{X}$$

The two present values are equal if:

$$(1 + r_f)^{-n} CE = (1 + k_0)^{-n} \bar{X}$$

Since $(1 + j) = \dfrac{\bar{X}}{CE}$ we obtain:

$$(1 + k_0)^n = (1 + j)(1 + r_f)^n$$

If r_f is constant, then j has to change if k_0 is constant through time.

Example:

The cash flow of X takes place in one year.

$r_f = .10$, $\bar{X} = \$1{,}320$, $CE = \$1{,}100$, $n = 1$

$$1 + j = \frac{1{,}320}{1{,}100} = 1.20.$$

The value of the risk adjusted discount rate k_0 is:

$$(1 + k_0)^n = (1 + j)(1 + r_f)^n$$

$$1 + k_0 = 1.20(1.10) = 1.32$$

$$k_0 = .32.$$

Applying the .32 discount rate to the expected cash flow:

$$PV = \frac{1{,}320}{1.32} = \$1{,}000.$$

Using the certainty equivalent method:

$$PV = \frac{1{,}100}{1.10} = \$1{,}000$$

Note that k_o depends on the value of n. If k_0 is constant the value of j for different time periods would have to change. For example, if $n = 2$ for k_o to be equal to .32 it is necessary for j to equal .44:

$$(1.32)^2 = (1 + j)(1.10)^2$$

$$j = .44$$

3. *Simulation*

When probability distributions are placed on different events, a straight mathematical solution can become difficult. A simulation of the outcomes enables us to obtain a probability distribution of outcomes. However, it is still necessary to interpret this probability distribution. This interpretation may be difficult. Outcomes are listed as a result of the simulation. But how is the decision to be made? Simulations result in a large amount of information, but the problem of how to make the decision still exists.

4. *Sensitivity Analysis*

Outcomes are determined for different assumptions. Sensitivity analysis allows us to determine the effect of changing a decision variable (such as price) or a computational variable (such as the discount rate) to see if the change affects the desirability of the investment. The process does not lead to an exact conclusion as to what the decision should be, but it does supply useful information. The problem of determining the discount rate still exists.

Hidden assumptions ("computer run number 86") may undermine one's faith in the results. Are the assumed variables chosen to achieve the needed profitability?

5. *Utility Analysis*

Whose utility function? People have utility functions, not corporations, therefore the theory is not easily applied. But expected monetary value is not a sufficient basis for making decisions.

Utility analysis is a fine technique except that it applies to an individual and not to a group or an organization such as a corporation. Also, there still remains the problem of coping with time value as well as risk.

The St. Petersburg Paradox is a famous example leading to a very large (infinite) expected monetary value for an investment having a very small market value. This illustrates well certain types of business decisions.

Consider a game with the following characteristics: Flip a fair coin until a "head". You will receive a payoff of 2^n where n is the number of tosses until the first head. How much would you pay?

If a head appears on the first toss the investor earns $2. If the first head appears on the second toss the investor receives $2^2 = \$4$. Since the lowest amount you will receive is $2 you will be willing to pay something more than $2. How much more than $2 will depend on your utility function. Table 1 shows the possible outcomes and their probabilities.

Since there is no limit to n, and each product of outcome and probability is $1, the expected monetary value, assuming an infinitely wealthy banker, is infinite.

Most of us would not pay a large sum to play this game. For example, if we paid $5 there would be .75 probability of losing, and only .25 probability of winning. If we paid $9 there would be 7/8 probability of losing and only 1/8 probability of winning. The

Table 1: St. Petersburg Paradox. Win 2^n

n	Outcomes 2^n	Probability	Expectation (Product)
1	2	1/2	1
2	4	1/4	1
3	8	1/8	1
4	16	1/16	1

fact that many very large outcomes with very low probabilities of occurring cause the expected value to be large, does not move us to be willing to pay large amounts for the game. In business, any investment with a very small probability of a very large profit but with a large probability of losing, becomes a form of St. Petersburg paradox.

6. *The Capital Asset Pricing Model (CAPM)*

Not all investors (or managers) are perfectly diversified. When managers are not diversified, the CAPM is a very poor guide for the managers to use in making decisions.

Figure 1 shows the required returns for different values of Beta (instead of Beta, the X axis could be measuring a more general measure of risk). The larger the amount of risk, the larger the required return (the WACC of the firm is the same for all levels of risk for individual investments).

Let r_m be the market return with variance σ_m^2 and define the risk of investment i to be:

$$\text{Beta} = \frac{\text{Cov}(r_i, r_m)}{\sigma_m^2}$$

The capital asset pricing model (CAPM) was for several years looked at as supplying a solution to decision making under uncertainty. Now we understand that the assumptions of the CAPM (perfectly diversified investors with quadratic utility functions or where the outcomes of the investment returns are normally distributed)

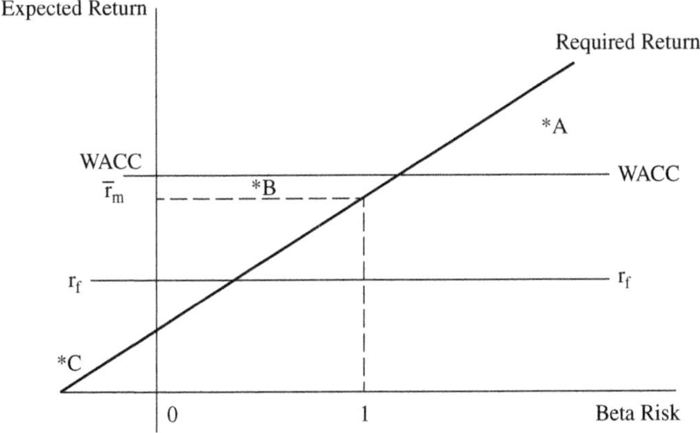

Figure 1:

may not be valid. In addition, the CAPM is a one period model and it is not clear that applying it to a multi-period investment is valid.

Most importantly, the CAPM focuses solely on systematic risk (the risk that the return will vary because of changes in the market return). The risks that are special to the specific investment being considered (the residual or unsystematic risk) are not relevant to the decisions. The majority of managers reject this assumption. They think unsystematic risk is relevant (unsystematic risk certainly affects management).

7. *Option Theory*

Additional elements are considered; these elements could be considered using a cash flow analysis, but the option theory approach focuses management's attention on the alternatives and the value of having alternatives.

Diversification

Diversification is one of the great tools of finance. Figure 2 shows that a good investment (with risk) combined with a bad investment

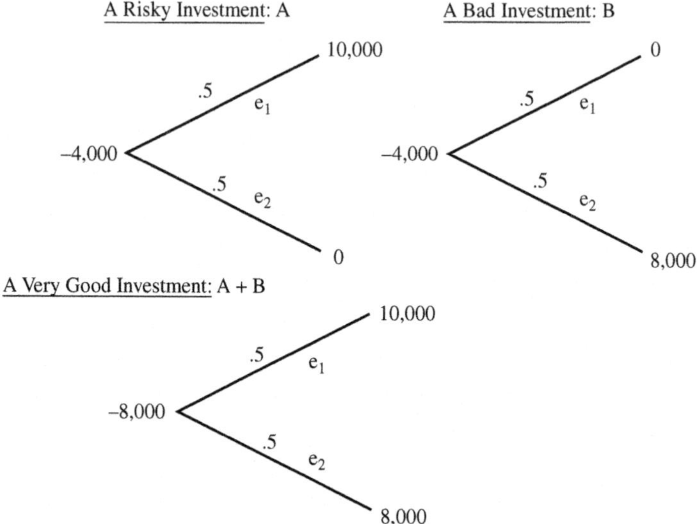

Figure 2: Risk: Portfolio Considerations

(with risk) can lead to a very good safe investment. The results of combining the two investments depends heavily on the way that the investment outcomes are correlated with each other.

Investment A has an expected value of \$1,000 and would be acceptable to a risk neutral investor. However, a risk averse investor might reject the opportunity to lose \$4,000 with a .5 probability.

Investment B has an expected monetary value of \$0 and only a person seeking risk would accept the investment. Most of us would reject B.

Now, consider what happens when both A and B are accepted. By accepting the bad investment B we eliminate the risk of A, and make it possible to accept A. While there remains a .5 probability of a zero net return, there is .5 probability of winning \$2,000 (net of the \$8,000 outlay). This is a desirable lottery since there is a probability of winning and zero probability of losing.

Investment B is negatively correlated with investment A. If event e_1 occurs you win with A and lose with B. If event e_2 occurs you lose with A but win with B. In the real world negatively correlated investments are difficult to find, but they do appear now and again. Life and fire insurance are two examples. If a firm is using a commodity, buying a futures contract for that commodity is negatively correlated with the future purchasing actions.

A more lengthy discussion of portfolio considerations would next consider what happens when the investments are perfectly dependent, independent of each other, or only partially correlated. The relationships of investments with each other greatly affects the amount of risk introduced by accepting an investment.

There are different levels of risk. We next show the underlying risk of an investment, the way the investment is correlated with other assets of the firm, and finally how the investment is correlated with the market. Finance theory says that only the third risk is relevant.

First, there is the basic risk of the proposed investment. What is the probability distribution of the outcomes? What is the spread or variance of outcomes? This risk is evaluated independently of other risks of the firm or how the returns of the investment are correlated with the market returns.

a. The basic risk of a proposed investment can be defined in terms of its variance.

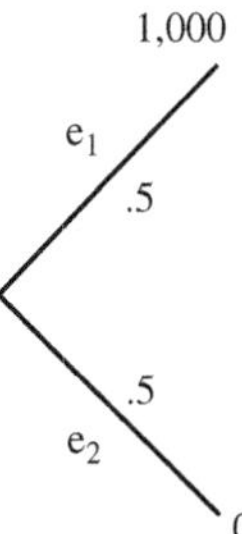

But logic says that the extent this investment is correlated with the firm's other investments is more important than the investment's specific risk.

The second risk consideration is how the investment being considered is correlated with other assets of the firm. This risk is particularly important to managers. They tend to want to reduce their firm's risk. This is accomplished by undertaking investments that have low correlation (or negative correlation) with the other assets of the firm.

b. How does the proposed investment correlate with the firm's other assets?

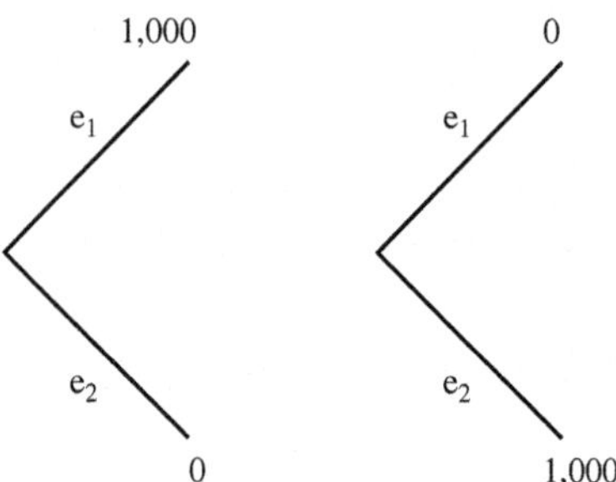

The third risk is important to well diversified investors. How is the investment being considered correlated with the returns of other investments? This risk is measured by the Beta of the investment.

c. But theory says the only relevant risk from the viewpoint of the well diversified investor is the correlation with the market What is its Beta?

Consider the above analysis from the viewpoint of a plant manager, a CEO, and a portfolio manager. Their goals are different. The plant manager is concerned with the variance of the outcomes. The CEO is concerned with the correlation of this specific investment with the other assets of the firm. The portfolio manager is concerned with how the investment affects the riskiness of the portfolio.

There are four risk factors to consider:

a. the risk of the investment considered in isolation of other investments
b. the portfolio effect of the investment on the total assets of the firm

c. the portfolio effect of the investment on the well-being of the several interested parties (stockholders, managers, workers, community, etc.)
d. the market risk adjustment.

Since investors in the firm can diversify their own portfolio and take steps to obtain the type of risk structure they prefer, it is not clear that the management of a corporation has to be greatly concerned with portfolio considerations of individual investors. From the point of view of the stockholders, management does not have to pay a large price for decreasing the variance of returns per dollar of assets. Having computed the present value of an investment that has reasonable probability of success, management does not have to deduct a large risk premium for the variance of the outcomes in the interests of the stockholders. However, the other interested parties might well want a large risk premium deducted for assets that increase the overall risk of the firm because of the risk characteristics of the investment considered in isolation or because of its portfolio effects. A practical approach is to have the person preparing information for the decision compute the expected present values for different interest rates, and indicate the present values. The more relevant rates are the default free rate, the borrowing rate, asset specific risk adjusted discount rates, and the firm's cost of capital. Information about how the investment's return would correlate with other assets and with the market should be clearly defined.

The separation of time value and risk adjustments is a necessity for making reasonable investment decisions. We can expect reluctance on the part of senior management to accept default free time value factors that are approximately one half of the rates that they are accustomed to using. However, the firm that insists on using time value factors that are excessively high will leave a lot of space for competitors to slip in.

It is not correct to assume that it is always appropriate to take the risk of an investment into account via the discounting (and compounding) procedure. There is no reason for assuming that risk is always compounded through time, and that $(1 + r)^{-n}$ can be used to take risk and time value factors into consideration in one computation.

Assume an investment is available that costs \$100,000,000 and promises to return either \$300,000,000 or \$0, the events both having .5 probability. The payoff occurs in a time period shortly after the outlay. The expected rate of return is thus very large. While this investment is "obviously" acceptable using the criterion "accept when the expected rate of return is greater than .10", it is not all clear that investors who are currently expecting a return of .10 for a moderately risky small firm would want this investment accepted because of the .5 probability of losing \$100,000,000.

If investors are well diversified, then certain types of risk are less important than other types of risk. In fact, with perfectly diversified investors, risks that are specific to the firm can be diversified away by the investor and thus are not relevant to the decision maker. The risk that is relevant to the investor is how the investment's return is correlated with the return of the other investments available to the investor.

This can be translated mathematically into an expression that allows us to quantify risk premiums. The inputs into the calculation are the measures of the market return risk trade-off (analogous to the use of the market interest rates to measure the time value factor), and a measure of the degree to which the profitability of the investment is correlated with the market return. Other problems arise in application because many investors are not perfectly diversified. Another complication is that there are other parties (such as managers) who have interest in the firm's continuity of existence, and we have to be careful to consider their welfare as well as the welfare of the common stockholders. Finally, the specific mathematical models only apply to certain limited probability distributions or utility functions.

Next we will consider a new simplified approach to evaluating investments when there is uncertainty.

A Simplified Discounting Rule (SDR)*

To obtain a solution to the very complex problem of evaluating investments under conditions of uncertainty we will make a simplifying assumption. We assume the asset's cash flow is a linear function of the market's return.

The following notation will be used.

Let

- X be the investment's annual cash flow
- r_f be the risk free rate (constant through time)
- r_m be the market return
- C_0 be the investment's cash flow if $1 + r_m = 0$
- C_f be the cash flow if the market earns r_f.
- b be the slope of the cash flow line where $b = \dfrac{C_f - C_0}{1 + r_f}$

A One Period Example

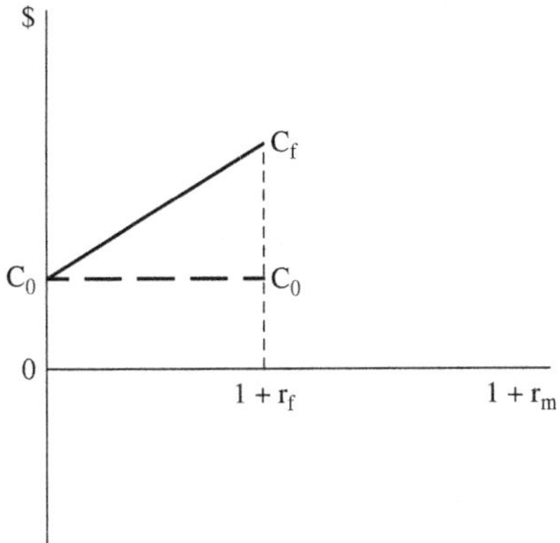

Cash Flow As A Function of $(1 + r_m)$

*Adapted from Fischer Black, "A Simple Discounting Rule," *Financial Management*, Summer 1988, pp. 7–11.

Assume the cash flow at time one is:

$$X = C_0 + \left(\frac{C_f - C_0}{1 + r_f}\right)(1 + r_m)$$

The present value is:

$$PV = \frac{C_0}{1 + r_f} + \frac{C_f - C_0}{1 + r_f}\left(\frac{1 + r_m}{1 + r_m}\right) = \frac{C_f}{1 + r_f}$$

The period can be of any length of time.

C_0 is discounted at the risk free rate (r_f) since C_0 has zero risk (this cash flow component is not correlated with r_m). The risky component $\frac{C_f - C_0}{1+r_f}(1 + r_m)$ is discounted at r_m, the market rate. The PV is $\frac{C_f}{1+r_f}$. The cash flow could be estimated assuming the market earns a return of r_f, and this cash flow is then discounted at r_f. The cash flow estimate and the discount rate are linked together. The primary problem is that if X is not related in a linear fashion to r_m the simple relationship does not hold.

Multi-Period Example

Let us assume that we want to value a cash flow at time n. Based on the above analysis the value at time $(n - 1)$ is

$$\frac{C_f}{1 + r_f}$$

and since this value is a certainty equivalent the value at time zero is

$$\frac{C_f}{(1 + r_f)^n}.$$

The Power of Compound Interest

The next example is aimed at illustrating the power of compound interest. Assume a paper is folded in half 50 times. The paper is $\frac{1}{450''}$ thick. How "thick" would the fold be?

Answer:

$\frac{1}{12}$ converts to feet

$\frac{1}{5280}$ converts to miles

2^{50} represents the folding in half 50 times

$$\frac{1}{450}\left(\frac{1}{12}\right)\left(\frac{1}{5280}\right)2^{50} = 39{,}500{,}000 \text{ miles}$$

Conclusions

There are two major errors in evaluating investments:

1. Do not have any faith in any calculations, and go "by the seat of the pants".
2. Make all decisions based on the "Accept or Reject" quantitative investment criteria with no qualitative considerations.

Bad capital budgeting techniques are a major handicap likely to prevent the achievement of corporate goals. Not undertaking good projects adds to the risk of a corporation.

Good capital budgeting techniques will enhance managerial capability; they are not a substitute for good management. Calculations are important, but consider the following:

> The real challenge is creativity and invention, not analysis. Timely execution of projects by entrepreneurial managers is also more critical than sophistication of analytical budgeting techniques.
>
> — A Vice President, Finance

Corporate practice has moved from the use of measures (payback and return on investment) that failed to consider effectively time value to an acceptance of discounted cash flow measure. While the cost of capital has been recommended as the discount rate or the hurdle rate to be used by firms, and was used by a large number of firms, the measure implicitly incorporated both time value and risk considerations, and the compound interest calculation using the weighted average cost of capital did not result in a reliable value measure.

A default free time value factor followed logically from the conclusion that risk did not necessarily compound through time. However, this left risk considerations out of the analysis. Sensitivity analysis and simulation, while giving useful insights, did not lead to explicit accept or reject recommendations. Finally, the capital asset pricing model was offered as a possible solution to the problem of how to include time value and risk. Unfortunately, the calculations require unrealistic assumptions and the model is not apt to apply to the specific investment of the firm being analyzed.

Despite the limitations of the capital asset pricing model, business managers should be knowledgeable of its characteristics. It offers a way of quantifying and incorporating risk considerations if the facts of the situation fit. Investments rejected under conventional analysis using the cost of capital might become acceptable, and investments previously considered to be acceptable might be rejected because of their "systematic" risk; that is, the risk that they will go down in value if the general market conditions deteriorate.

Too frequently managers have been unnecessarily confused about the basic nature of the net present value and the internal rate of return methods, thus reluctant to use them. The DCF calculations are powerful tools for evaluating investments. While the uncertainty questions occupy the academic literature, the operating business person should realize that the basic DCF calculations are still the most reliable ways of evaluating investments, and are an important tool in deciding whether or not an investment is acceptable. While we do not have exact decision rules when there is uncertainty, there are known methods of analysis that are useful in coping with investment decision making under uncertainty.

Lecture 29

Reflections on Management Education and Management

Date and occasion are unknown.

This evening I will reflect on two aspects of life and career that deserve periodic review and evaluation.

The first aspect is directly important to those of us who teach management, and indirectly important to all. This is the subject of education for management. I will discuss five things that all management schools teach reasonably well.

1. Fundamental theories and rules of thumb. Consider some samples:
   - Marginal and incremental analysis. Do not use average cost without a lot of fear.
   - Opportunity cost principle. The alternative use determines relevant cost for decisions.
   - Sunk costs are never relevant. Exceptions: tax calculation and regulation.
   - Comparative advantage. Relative values of resources should affect their use. You do not want your 7'4" center dribbling the ball downcourt, even if he is the best dribbler.
   - Portfolio theory. Diversification of risk. Decision theory.
   - The quantification of time discounting. A dollar today is worth more than a dollar received tomorrow.

Professors like to teach theories, and even complex theories are useful. Consider the statement by H.L. Mencken:

> "For every complex and difficult issue, there is always an answer that is simple, easy, and wrong!"

Despite the above, rules of thumb and wisdoms do have their use.

The wisdoms taught at a business school range from the Ben Franklin statement, "a penny saved is a penny earned," to the equally famous, "there is no such thing as a free lunch". One professor has taught for years that you should "plan before you act", and a second professor has argued that you should "act instead of plan". In finance "buy low, sell high" is good advice but "buy low, sell if it goes lower" is better advice.

Wisdoms are inexact guides. For example "a stitch in time saves nine" is good advice. On the other hand if one translates the wisdom into operational practice there is generally a problem. What does a stitch cost and what are the benefits? What is the probability of the stitch being needed and if so, when will it be needed? For many wisdoms there are equal and opposite wisdoms. For example, compare "any job worth doing is worth doing well", with the statement "any job worth doing, is worth doing badly". The reasoning of the former statement is that an important task must be done and not put off.

Wisdoms are fun and sometimes useful. Generally they are not subject to empirical tests, and frequently the wisdoms of yesterday become the discarded myths of today. One has to be careful of "wisdoms" and "rules of thumb" and judge their usefulness in today's environment compared to the theories that are currently available.

Continuing with the list of things that management schools teach reasonably well:

2. Institutional considerations.

- Tax laws
- Trade agreements
- Anti-trust laws

Many professors do not like to teach institutional considerations, and this information has a finite life.

3. Model building (and its limitations) and problem solving.
   - Finance, Operations, Marketing heavily depend on models, and the teaching of problem solving relies on case.
4. Skills and Languages of Business.
   - Accounting
   - Computers
   - Written and oral communication skills (we know how to improve these skills, we do not know how to make students great communicators).
5. Knowledge of Markets, People, and Organizations.
   - International considerations.
   - Self interest motivates and when properly harnessed can increase social welfare.
   - Maximize and satisfice. More income is better, but don't search eternally for the perfect solution.
   - How to manage people and organizations.
   - How to develop strategies.

There are also at least five important things that management schools do less well:

1. Teach students how to learn (think).
2. Teach students how to be leaders.
3. Teach students how to innovate.
4. Teach students how to be personable, intelligent, dedicated, ethical, happy, and nice. How to interact with others and how to manage.
5. Teach students how to be outstanding in all the areas that the schools teach well.

A teacher asked a student "Who was Socrates?" The student responded "Socrates was a Greek philosopher and teacher who gave students good advice. They poisoned him."

One might think that business education should be teaching "how to manage", for this is the most important of all managerial subjects. But it is also difficult to teach management. There will be a tendency for professors in schools of management to teach what they know in those areas where progress in learning is relatively easily discernible. Thus we can expect the teaching of well-established theories, skills, wisdoms, markets, and institutional facts. The intangible skill of how to manage is apt to suffer in comparison until such time as major educational breakthroughs are established in this area.

Thus the present state of management education tends to neglect the important, for the feasible. But maybe this situation is reasonable; the principle of comparative advantage can be invoked to explain the present situation. Professors are at their best explaining theories, institutional facts, and skills. Life and experience teach many things leading to effective management, but life does not teach theory and complex skills.

Despite having admitted our limitations in teaching how to manage, as my second topic I will offer ten rules for achieving managerial success. All the rules are obvious, but they are all too often neglected.

Ten Rules for Achieving Managerial Success

1. Attend to the unglamorous but important details (if not yourself, then assign someone).
2. Set priorities and act based on the priorities.
3. Delegate but retain control and monitor performance.
4. Be decisive and make decisions where feasible (do not study opportunities until the opportunities disappear).
5. Be flexible and adjust to events (annual capital budgets lack flexibility). Have contingency plans.
6. Plan but do not use planning as a substitute for actions.
7. Seek, listen to and evaluate advice and ideas.

8. Pick talent that complements your abilities. Do not be afraid of people who are "better" than you.
9. Give credit generously and assign blame discretely.
10. Don't be locked into actions based on rigid thinking or obsolete rules. The order to "think" is one of the all-time great commands. Be willing to experiment.

Relative to "rigid thinking" consider the following famous quotation from Ralph Waldo Emerson:

> "A foolish consistency is the hobgoblin of little minds, adored by little statesmen and philosophers and divines. With consistency a great soul has simply nothing to do."

And also from Emerson relative to being a decisive decision maker:

> "In every work of genius we recognize our own rejected thoughts: they come back to us with a certain alienated majesty...tomorrow a stranger will say with masterly good sense precisely what we have thought and felt all the time, and we shall be forced to take with shame our own opinion from another."

As a guide for how to live your life we have:

> "The dice of God are always loaded. The world looks like a multiplication-table or a mathematical equation, which, turn it how you will, balances itself...Every secret is told, every crime is punished, every virtue rewarded, every wrong redressed, in silence and certainty."

And by Florence M. Kelso we have:

> "You buy the stock, you own the store.
> Free enterprisers laud it.
> But no one listens when I say
> More dividends, and by the way
> Because my son's a C.P.A.
> Let's have him do our audit."

I will end with three final quotations. They are relevant to all of us. First,

> "Most people cannot see beyond their self-interest to see their self-interest."

And from Thomas Jefferson:

"Reason and free inquiry are the only effectual agents against error."

Goya (Los Caprichos) said the same thought more strongly:

"The sleep of reason brings forth monsters."

Lecture 30

Ten Financial Money Makers for a Corporation

The paper has no date but it looks like early 1990. It fits most anywhere.

1. Capital Structure

   $$\text{Debt} + \text{CS} > \text{PS} + \text{CS}$$

   Conclusions:

   1. Use debt
   2. Use PS only if
      a. Zero tax
      b. Acquisitions
      c. Public utility
2. Hybrids: Use of convertible debt (common stock with a tax deduction) and convertible-exchanged preferred stock.
3. Retained savings versus dividends and new capital.
   Stock acquisition versus dividends
   Conclusion: Define a financial personality (dividends, capital structure, investment)
4. Pension payment timing is important.
5. Buy versus lease analysis can be done properly.
6. MLP
7. Size of bond issue is an optimizing decision
   $k_{long} > k_{short}$ issue minimum but solve for optimum
   $k_{short} > k_{long}$ Issue maximum

8. Credit granting decisions are "marginal" decisions.
9. Bond retirement and refunding decisions.
10. Make "correct" capital budgeting (efficiency and expansion) decisions.
    a. Mutually exclusive (IRR & NPV)
    b. Payback & ROI
    c. Risk adjusted rates
    d. Inflation
    e. Cost of RE versus New Capital
    f. Exclusion of debt flows
11. Mergers and Acquisitions and LBOs.

    (Note that eleven points have been listed. Subtract the one with which you disagree.)

Lecture 31

A Strategy for Management Education at the Johnson School

While aimed at the Johnson School, the recommendations are applicable to any school of management.

In February 1980 I was asked by representatives of the Class of 1980 to present the graduation address in May. If you graduated in May 1980, you do not remember my address. In April of 1980, I was told that they had made arrangements with a more impressive speaker so they would have to withdraw the invitation. I now gain my revenge.

My initial intention was to give two lectures. Ann vetoed that idea, so I flipped a coin and the lecture titled "A Corporate Tax Reform Act" will have to wait for another occasion.

As advertised, the talk you will hear is a strategy for management education at the Johnson School.

The first step is to reject false goals. These false goals include the seeking of an instant reputation obtained by hiring stars, a search for the unique educational gimmick, and an excessive concern for the ranking of the school where the ranking is made by persons who do not know the school. I advocate patience in faculty recruiting, teaching the fundamental theories, skills, and functional areas, and instead of reacting to rankings, review what we are doing and correct the deficiencies.

The second step is to avoid two extremes, both of which will lead to faulty educations. At one extreme is excessive reliance on immediate real world relevance and an ignoring of good theoretical foundations. The second extreme to avoid is an excessive amount of theory with no attempt to relate the theory to real world applications and complexities. I think we do a good job of avoiding both extremes.

As we search for excellence in the future, let us not forget those things that have led to our successes in the past. Above all, remember, we have been successful in the past. The quality of our MBA program has consistently been more than competitive with those of any school. It is entirely possible that we have had the best MBA program in the country for the last 30 years.

In the past, professors have balanced a concern for teaching with a concern for teaching with a concern for research. A professor seeking promotion at the Johnson School would be ill-advised to adopt a strategy of trying to be less than outstanding in either area.

Since I arrived at Cornell, I have seen graduating classes in our School grow from 90 to 250, and typical class enrollment increase from 20 to 90. I see no educational or financial advantage from size, and will be disappointed if there is not a substantive shrinkage in the size of the student body. With our prime competitors all nearing or breaking 1,000, we would do well to go in the other direction. Small size and concern for individual students could be our attainable uniqueness.

Since I have been at Cornell, the Business School's open door policy has been a fact. Professors are in their office and are accessible to students. This is not always true at our competitor schools. But the open door policy is fragile and may be inconsistent with a large student body. I hope it continues and that the Dean encourages the faculty to continue it. To have a quality institution, professors must be willing to "waste" time. It may be the most important thing they do. I do not want to be told that one can be more efficient away from the office. Efficiency measured in terms of pages of journal articles is a bad measure of efficiency.

Let us shift our attention to the need for resources. An excellent MBA program loses money with each student in attendance. Gifts and endowments are needed to sustain excellence.

For the School to achieve excellence, donors must trust the Dean. They can weaken a school by leaving the school financially worse off after the gift by requiring that the school do things it would otherwise not do, and which cost more than the gift. Donors should place a minimum of restrictions on how the funds are spent if the objective is to help the school.

I will define a simple understandable objective for the Johnson School. We want to make this a school where you would be pleased to have your children and grandchildren attend. A school where they will receive an education for the first job and for the job they will hold 40 years after starting their careers.

Lecture 32

Management of Risk and Capital Budgeting (1992)

This talk should be of interest to anyone working with the capital budgeting decision. A similar talk was given at the Johnson School and has been included earlier in this book.

After the management of a firm has completed its planning process, the resulting long range strategic plan has to be translated into a specific plan of action which actually allocates resources. I will call the specific plan to allocate resources the capital budget and capital budgeting is the process of arriving at the plan.

It is convenient to divide investments into two general classifications. First we classify all investment opportunities that are economically independent of each other. Thus an automobile manufacturer might consider replacing its automobile production line with a more labor efficient set of machines, or it might consider entering the airline industry. These are two independent investment alternatives. They compete for financial resources, but their cash flows are economically independent.

Once we have determined the independent investments we must next consider all investments which perform the same economic function, where only one investment will be accepted. These are "mutually exclusive" investments.

The objective of the capital budgeting process is to make accept or reject decisions involving independent investments (we can undertake all independent investments that are desirable) and "best of the set" decisions involving mutually exclusive investments (we can undertake only one of the mutually exclusive investments). In making these investment decisions there is implied some known and agreed upon objective for the firm.

As a first step we should clearly indicate the corporate objectives that are not affecting the capital budgeting process. We are not attempting to maximize total sales or percentage share of market. Growth is not the goal (though growth might occur if the correct decisions are made) nor are earnings per share and total earnings being maximized. The goal is to maximize the risk adjusted net present value of the stockholders' position and we assume that in doing so we are maximizing the well-being of the stockholders. The decisions are being made from the point of view of the stockholders and it is assumed that their interests are best served by a procedure that systematically assigns a cost to the capital that is utilized in the production process.

The capital budgeting process that is recommended must take into consideration a cost on the capital that is being utilized or more generally we can say that the process must take into consideration the time value of money. In addition, the process must also cope with the existence of uncertainty and adjust the analysis for the risk of the project being considered.

Capital budgeting decisions generally involve immediate (or nearly immediate) outlays and benefits that stretch out through time. In some cases the benefits may be deferred for many years. The primary problem facing management responsible for making capital budgeting decisions is to incorporate time value and risk considerations in such a manner that the well-being of the stockholders is maximized. There are no known simple and exact solutions to this problem.

Decision Pitfalls

There are several different types of pitfalls associated with capital budgeting decision procedures. For example, a firm can use an incorrect calculation method. Secondly, the firm can use a correct calculation method, but can use it incorrectly. Third, a firm can have a correct method of evaluating investments, but can evaluate managerial performance incorrectly, and this affects investment decisions. To illustrate the above, consider the following three relevant questions:

a. Does your firm use ROI (with other measures) to evaluate investments?
b. Does your firm use <u>one</u> "hurdle rate" or "required return"?
c. Is a division that earns .25 ROI in a year doing better than a division that earns .15? Assume the firm has a .10 cost of money.

"Yes" answers to questions a, b, or c are not acceptable. Let us first consider question a.

If the ROI calculation is based on conventional accounting, it cannot be used effectively to evaluate investments. The ROI measures used to evaluate investments are apt to be misleading since they leave out the time value of money effects.

Consider the following two investments:

	Cash Flows at Time:		
	0	1	2
Investment A	−10,000	1,000	11,000
Investment B	−10,000	11,000	1,000

A casual inspection of the above table reveals that the second investment is to be preferred to the first (the total amount received is the same for both investments, but the second investment receives some cash earlier than the first). The ROI method of evaluating investments will fail to reveal the superiority of B compared to A. For example, the total income over the life of either investment is $2,000 and the average income is $1,000 for an average investment of $5,000. This is a 20% return on investment (ROI) and both investments have this return. The ROI measure does not detect the superiority of B. Alternative ROI measures (e.g. using the ROI's of each year) would also fail to indicate the superiority of B compared to A. ROI as conventionally computed should not be used to evaluate investments.

ROI is an incorrect investment calculation method (flawed from a theoretical viewpoint).

The problem with using one hurdle rate or required return to take into consideration both the time value of money and risk is that each investment alternative is likely to have different risks in different time periods. Using one required return is likely to lead to the rejection of good (safe) investments and the acceptance of bad (risky) investments. While net present value (NPV) is a theoretically correct calculation method, if the discount rate being used is not an accurate representation of the cost of money, the results of the calculations may not be reliable. NPV would be a correct method being used incorrectly.

When is a lower ROI more desirable than a higher ROI? Assume the following facts apply.

	.15 Division	**.25 Division**
Capital Assets	$2,000,000,000	$500,000,000
Income	300,000,000	125,000,000
ROI	.15	.25

But consider:

	.15 Division	**.25 Division**
Income	$300,000,000	$125,000,000
Less:		
Interest Cost (.10)	200,000,000	50,000,000
Net Economic Income	$100,000,000	$75,000,000

The .15 division is contributing more "income" and is doing better for the firm than the .25 division. A firm that uses ROI to measure performance has introduced the likelihood that desirable investments will be rejected so that the firm's (or division's) performance will be enhanced. A firm can have a correct method of evaluating investments, but if ROI (or the equivalent) is used to measure managerial performance, this can adversely affect the quality of the decisions being made.

Capital Budgeting

Among the things we know about capital budgeting are:

a. NPV and IRR can both be used to evaluate correctly independent investments. The present value profile is a very useful method of presenting alternatives.
b. Mutually exclusive investment decisions are easily solved using NPV and may be solved equally correctly, but with more difficulty using IRR.
c. Payback (used with care) supplies some information concerning risk, but should not be the primary method used.
d. ROI (do not use). A stockholder should pay money to keep this measure of investment desirability off the decision maker's desk.

But consider the following from a Fortune 500 top manager:[1] "We use several different financial measures in evaluating investment proposals including Internal Rate of Return (IRR), Discounted Payback, Profitability Index, and "Proof Year" Operating Return on Investment."

Note the use of ROI and the exclusion of NPV. This is troublesome. ROI is used extensively (as a secondary method of evaluation) by major industrial firms to evaluate investments. This is a major deficiency in the quality of investment decision making.

The two issues for which there are not easily applied accepted solutions are:

a. Capital rationing which is caused by:

 Scarce resources (e.g. engineering talent)
 Scarce money (solutions are a programming problem or "beauty" contest)

The scarce resource problem may be easily solved by adjusting the input cost measure for the resource. The scarce money situation can theoretically be solved by a programming solution, but the

[1]The quotations are from H. Bierman, *Implementation of Capital Budgeting Techniques*, Financial Management Association, Tampa, Florida, 1986.

information requirements are immense, and the information is not likely to be readily available to management. Ad hoc solutions using IRR or the index of profitability are not reliable. Judgment (or a beauty contest) is not a bad alternative method of solution. Investments would still have to satisfy the NPV or IRR criteria.

The remainder of the talk will deal with capital budgeting under uncertainty.

b. Uncertainty-Risk

When we consider the uncertainty problem, the need for exact solutions for capital rationing situations is greatly reduced, since the underlying uncertainties are so important.

Uncertainty

The largest number of business decisions are made under conditions of uncertainty. Unfortunately, there are no easy answers or simple formulas that can be applied with exactness when the outcomes are uncertain. We will define uncertainty to exist when more than one outcome is possible. The uncertainty becomes burdensome when one or more of the possible outcomes are undesirable. We call this risk. If we can win either \$1,000,000 or \$2,000,000 there is uncertainty. If we can either win \$1,000,000 or lose \$50,000 there is risk.

A primary problem that complicates the analysis is that the relative importance of the time value adjustment and the risk adjustment will vary among investments that have the same type of risk but with the cash flows occurring in different time periods. The implication of this is that the use of one risk adjusted discount rate to evaluate all investments, or even to evaluate all the cash flows of one investment is likely to give misleading results.

The practical problems of capital budgeting under uncertainty are highlighted by the following statement by a Fortune 100 manager:

> In addition to organizational complexity, we are faced with capital budgeting lead times for new technology capacity that often exceed the horizon of our strategic planning process for individual products. Occasionally, we are investing in capacity to house machinery and

equipment that has not been invented that will produce products not yet on the drawing boards of the product development divisions. Clearly, the uncertainties and risks of this environment make analytical analysis of capital budgeting an art at best.

Director, Financial Analysis

Rather than one solution, I propose the following methods of coping with uncertainty:

1. Payback and WACC
2. Risk adjusted discount rates
3. Simulation
   (listing outcomes)
   Monte Carlo
4. Sensitivity analysis
   (change the value of the variables)
5. Utility analysis
6. CAPM
7. Option Theory
8. A Simplified Discounting Rule

1. Payback and WACC

What payback period is required? Should the required payback period depend on the life of the investment or the timing of the cash flows? Payback can be used to give an impression of risk or safety, but it cannot be used as a general measure of profitability.

The weighted average cost of capital (WACC) is an average return that is a reasonable overall target for the firm but tells us little about whether a specific investment should be undertaken.

Note the word average in "Weighted <u>Average</u> Cost of Capital". Can you apply an average cost of capital to an unique investment? It is likely that the WACC should not be applied to the specific investment whose value is being calculated because the risk (or cash flow) characteristics are not average.

2. Risk Adjusted Discount Rates

The most widely used method is the risk adjusted discount rate. If a safe investment must earn .10, a risky investment must be expected to earn more. The procedure is easy to implement, but it is very difficult to analyze exactly what is being accomplished. Does risk increase exponentially through time? This is implied by the use of $(1 + j)^{-n}$ where j is a risk adjusted discount rate. The mix of time and risk leading to one discount rate used for investments with different lives is not a reliable process.

Consider the following example. With a .07 discount rate the firm needs $224.23 at time 80 to have $1 of present value. How many $ do you need, at time 80, r = .25, to have $1 of present value?

Future Values

r/n	**1**	**20**	**80**
.07	1.07	3.87	224.23
.15	1.15		
.25	1.25		?

The answer to the question is $\$1(1.25)^{80} = \$56{,}597{,}994$. The present value of $56,597,994 received at time 80 is $1 if the appropriate discount rate is .25. Conclusion: The combination of time value and risk in one calculation is not a reliable process. If the .25 interest rate represents the borrowing rate for the firm, then $56,597,994 is too low an estimate of the cash flows needed. If the firm's borrowing rate is .08 and there is a .17 risk adjustment for planting safe trees then probably $56,597,994 is too large. The amount needed for a safe investment is only $\$1(1.08)^{80} = \$772$.

Under what circumstances can we assume that the use of $(1{+}r)^{-n}$ is correct even if r includes a risk premium? The risk discount (difference between the expected value and certainty equivalent) has to be changing through time.

Certainty equivalents are very attractive in that they are easy to work with, and it might appear that we know what we are doing. But we do not know how to obtain systematically certainty equivalents.

We want to relate certainty equivalents and risk adjusted discount rates.

Let:

CE	be the certainty equivalent of the cash flow X
$\bar{X}$	be the expected cash flow
k_o	be the risk adjusted discount rate
r_f	be the risk free rate
j	be the certainty equivalent conversion factor:

$$1 + j = \frac{\bar{X}}{CE}$$

The present value of a cash flow with a certainty equivalent of CE occurring at time n is:

$$PV = (1 + r_f)^{-n} CE$$

If the expected value and the risk adjusted discount rate is used, the present value is:

$$PV = (1 + k_0)^{-n} \bar{X}$$

The two present values are equal if:

$$(1 + r_f)^{-n} CE = (1 + k_0)^{-n} \bar{X}$$

Since $(1 + j) = \frac{\bar{X}}{CE}$ we obtain:

$$(1 + k_0)^n = (1 + j)(1 + r_f)^n$$

If r_f is constant, then j has to change if k_0 is constant through time.

Example:

The cash flow of X takes place in one year.

$$r_f = .10, \bar{X} = \$1{,}320, CE = \$1{,}100, n = 1$$
$$1 + j = \frac{1{,}320}{1{,}100} = 1.20.$$

The value of the risk adjusted discount rate k_0 is:

$$(1 + k_0)^n = (1 + j)(1 + r_f)^n$$
$$1 + k_0 = 1.20(1.10) = 1.32$$
$$k_0 = .32.$$

Applying the .32 discount rate to the expected cash flow:

$$\mathrm{PV} = \frac{1{,}320}{1.32} = \$1{,}000.$$

Using the certainty equivalent method:

$$\mathrm{PV} = \frac{1{,}100}{1.10} = \$1{,}000$$

Note that k_0 depends on the value of n. If k_0 is constant the value of j for different time periods would have to change. For example, if $n = 2$ for k_0 to be equal to .32 it is necessary for j to equal .44:

$$(1.32)^2 = (1 + j)(1.10)^2$$
$$j = .44$$

3. Simulation

When probability distributions are placed on different events, a straight mathematical solution can become difficult. A simulation of the outcomes enables us to obtain a probability distribution of outcomes. However, it is still necessary to interpret this probability distribution. This interpretation may be difficult. Outcomes are listed as a result of the simulation. But how is the decision to be made? Simulations result in a large amount of information, but the problem of how to make the decision still exists.

4. Sensitivity analysis

Outcomes are determined for different assumptions. Sensitivity analysis allows us to determine the effect of changing a decision variable (such as price) or a computational variable (such as the discount rate) to see if the change affects the desirability of the investment. The process does not lead to an exact conclusion as to what the decision should be, but it does supply useful information. The problem of determining the discount rate still exists.

Hidden assumptions ("computer run number 86") may undermine one's faith in the results. Are the assumed variables chosen to achieve the needed profitability?

Table 1: St. Petersburg Paradox Win 2^n

n	Outcomes 2^n	Probability	Expectation (Product)
1	2	1/2	1
2	4	1/4	1
3	8	1/8	1
4	16	1/16	1

5. Utility analysis

Whose utility function? People have utility functions, not corporations, therefore the theory is not easily applied. But expected monetary value is not a sufficient basis for making decisions.

Utility analysis is a fine technique except that it applies to an individual and not to a group or an organization such as a corporation. Also, there still remains the problem of coping with time value as well as risk.

The St. Petersburg Paradox is a famous example leading to a very large (infinite) expected monetary value for an investment having a very small market value. This illustrates well certain types of business decisions.

Consider a game with the following characteristics: Flip a fair coin until a "head". You will receive a payoff of 2^n where n is the number of tosses until the first head. How much would you pay?

If a head appears on the first toss the investor earns \$2. If the first head appears on the second toss the investor receives $2^2 = \$4$. Since the lowest amount you will receive is \$2 you will be willing to pay something more than \$2. How much more than \$2 will depend on your utility function. The following table shows the possible outcomes and their probabilities.

Since there is no limit to n, and each product of outcome and probability is \$1, the expected monetary value, assuming an infinitely wealthy banker, is infinite.

Most of us would not pay a large sum to play this game. For example, if we paid \$5 there would be .75 probability of losing, and only .25 probability of winning. If we paid \$9 there would be

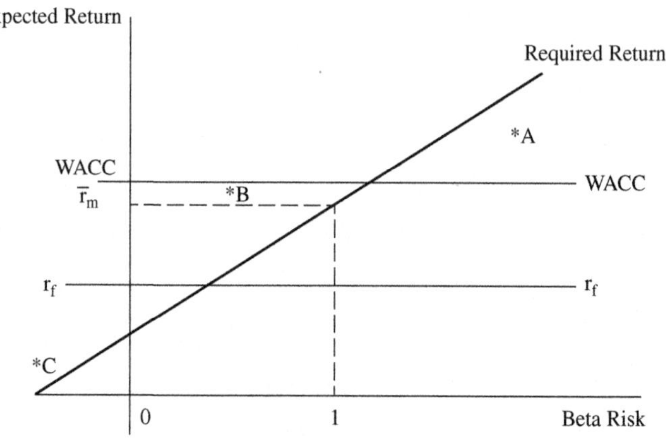

Figure 1:

7/8 probability of losing and only 1/8 probability of winning. The fact that many very large outcomes with very low probabilities of occurring cause the expected value to be large, does not move us to be willing to pay large amounts for the game. In business, any investment with a very small probability of a very large profit but with a large probability of losing, becomes a form of St. Petersburg paradox.

6. The capital asset pricing model (CAPM)

Not all investors (or managers) are perfectly diversified. When managers are not diversified, the CAPM is a very poor guide for the managers to use in making decisions.

Figure 1 shows the required returns for different values of Beta (instead of Beta, the X axis could be measuring a more general measure of risk). The larger the amount of risk, the larger the required return (the WACC of the firm is the same for all levels of risk for individual investments).

Let r_m be the market return with variance σ_m^2 and define the risk of investment i to be:

$$\text{Beta} = \frac{\text{Cov}(r_i, r_m)}{\sigma_m^2}$$

The capital asset pricing model (CAPM) was for several years looked at as supplying a solution to decision making under uncertainty. Now we understand that the assumptions of the CAPM (perfectly diversified investors with quadratic utility functions or where the outcomes of the investment returns are normally distributed) may not be valid. In addition, the CAPM is a one period model and it is not clear that applying it to a multi-period investment is valid.

Most importantly, the CAPM focuses solely on systematic risk (the risk that the return will vary because of changes in the market return). The risks that are special to the specific investment being considered (the residual or unsystematic risk) are not relevant to the decisions. The majority of managers reject this assumption. They think unsystematic risk is relevant (unsystematic risk certainly affects management).

7. Option Theory

Additional elements are considered; these elements could be considered using a cash flow analysis, but the option theory approach focuses management's attention on the alternatives and the value of having alternatives.

Diversification

Diversification is one of the great tools of finance. Figure 2 shows that a good investment (with risk) combined with a bad investment (with risk) can lead to a very good safe investment. The results of combining the two investments depends heavily on the way that the investment outcomes are correlated with each other.

Investment A has an expected value of \$1,000 and would be acceptable to a risk neutral investor. However, a risk averse investor might reject the opportunity to lose \$4,000 with a .5 probability.

Investment B has an expected monetary value of \$0 and only a person seeking risk would accept the investment. Most of us would reject B.

Now, consider what happens when both A and B are accepted. By accepting the bad investment B we eliminate the risk of A, and make it possible to accept A. While there remains a .5 probability of

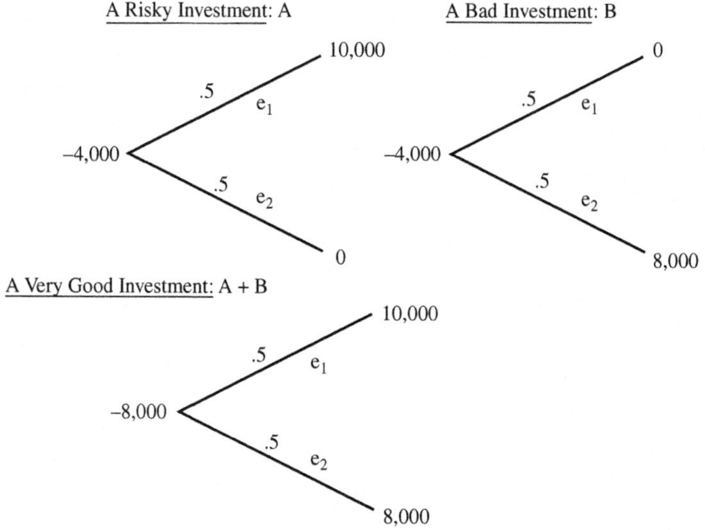

Figure 2: Risk: Portfolio Considerations

a zero net return, there is .5 probability of winning $2,000 (net of the $8,000 outlay). This is a desirable lottery since there is a probability of winning and zero probability of losing.

Investment B is negatively correlated with investment A. If event e_1 occurs you win with A and lose with B. If event e_2 occurs you lose with A but win with B. In the real world negatively correlated investments are difficult to find, but they do appear now and again. Life and fire insurance are two examples. If a firm is using a commodity, buying a futures contract for that commodity is negatively correlated with the future purchasing actions.

A more lengthy discussion of portfolio considerations would next consider what happens when the investments are perfectly dependent, independent of each other, or only partially correlated. The relationships of investments with each other greatly affects the amount of risk introduced by accepting an investment.

There are different levels of risk. We next show the underlying risk of an investment, the way the investment is correlated with other assets of the firm, and finally how the investment is correlated with the market. Finance theory says that only the third risk is relevant.

First, there is the basic risk of the proposed investment. What is the probability distribution of the outcomes? What is the spread or variance of outcomes? This risk is evaluated independently of other risks of the firm or how the returns of the investment are correlated with the market returns.

a. The basic risk of a proposed investment can be defined in terms of its variance.

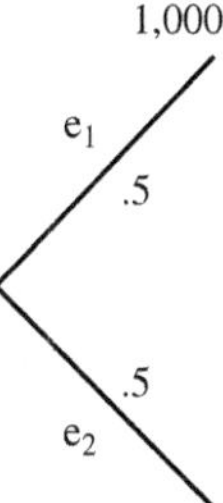

But logic says that the extent this investment is correlated with the firm's other investments is more important than the investment's specific risk.

The second risk consideration is how the investment being considered is correlated with other assets of the firm. This risk is particularly important to managers. They tend to want to reduce their firm's risk. This is accomplished by undertaking investments that have low correlation (or negative correlation) with the other assets of the firm.

b. How does the proposed investment correlate with the firm's other assets?

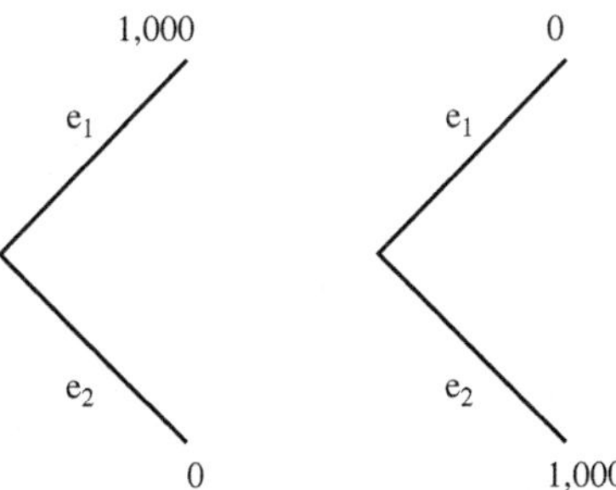

The third risk is important to well diversified investors. How is the investment being considered correlated with the returns of other investments? This risk is measured by the Beta of the investment.

c. But theory says the only relevant risk from the viewpoint of the well diversified investor is the correlation with the market. What is its Beta?

Consider the above analysis from the viewpoint of a plant manager, a CEO, and a portfolio manager. Their goals are different. The plant manager is concerned with the variance of the outcomes. The CEO is concerned with the correlation of this specific investment with the other assets of the firm. The portfolio manager is concerned with how the investment affects the riskiness of the portfolio.

There are four risk factors to consider:

a. the risk of the investment considered in isolation of other investments
b. the portfolio effect of the investment on the total assets of the firm
c. the portfolio effect of the investment on the well-being of the several interested parties (stockholders, managers, workers, community, etc.)
d. the market risk adjustment.

Since investors in the firm can diversify their own portfolio and take steps to obtain the type of risk structure they prefer, it is not clear that the management of a corporation has to be greatly concerned with portfolio considerations of individual investors. From the point of view of the stockholders, management does not have to pay a large price for decreasing the variance of returns per dollar of assets. Having computed the present value of an investment that has reasonable probability of success, management does not have to deduct a large risk premium for the variance of the outcomes in the interests of the stockholders. However, the other interested parties might well want a large risk premium deducted for assets that increase the overall risk of the firm because of the risk characteristics of the investment considered in isolation or because of its portfolio effects. A practical approach is to have the person preparing information for the decision compute the expected present values for different interest rates, and indicate the present values. The more relevant rates are the default free rate, the borrowing rate, asset specific risk adjusted discount rates, and the firm's cost of capital. Information about how the investment's return would correlate with other assets and with the market should be clearly defined.

The separation of time value and risk adjustments is a necessity for making reasonable investment decisions. We can expect reluctance on the part of senior management to accept default free time value factors that are approximately one half of the rates that they are accustomed to using. However, the firm that insists on using time value factors that are excessively high will leave a lot of space for competitors to slip in.

It is not correct to assume that it is always appropriate to take the risk of an investment into account via the discounting (and compounding) procedure. There is no reason for assuming that risk is always compounded through time, and that $(1 + \mathrm{r})^{-\mathrm{n}}$ can be used to take risk and time value factors into consideration in one computation.

Assume an investment is available that costs $100,000,000 and promises to return either $300,000,000 or $0, the events both having .5 probability. The payoff occurs in a time period shortly after the outlay. The expected rate of return is thus very large. While this investment is "obviously" acceptable using the criterion "accept when the expected rate of return is greater than .10", it is not all clear that investors who are currently expecting a return of .10 for a moderately risky small firm would want this investment accepted because of the .5 probability of losing $100,000,000.

If investors are well diversified, then certain types of risk are less important than other types of risk. In fact, with perfectly diversified investors, risks that are specific to the firm can be diversified away by the investor and thus are not relevant to the decision maker. The risk that is relevant to the investor is how the investment's return is correlated with the return of the other investments available to the investor.

This can be translated mathematically into an expression that allows us to quantify risk premiums. The inputs into the calculation are the measures of the market return risk trade-off (analogous to the use of the market interest rates to measure the time value factor), and a measure of the degree to which the profitability of the investment is correlated with the market return. Other problems arise in application because many investors are not perfectly diversified. Another complication is that there are other parties (such as managers) who have interest in the firm's continuity of existence, and we have to be careful to consider their welfare as well as the welfare of the common stockholders. Finally, the specific mathematical models only apply to certain limited probability distributions or utility functions.

Next we will consider a new simplified approach to evaluating investments when there is uncertainty.

A Simplified Discounting Rule (SDR)*

To obtain a solution to the very complex problem of evaluating investments under conditions of uncertainty we will make a simplifying assumption. We assume the asset's cash flow is a linear function of the market's return.

The following notation will be used.

Let

X be the investment's annual cash flow

r_f be the risk free rate (constant through time)

r_m be the market return

C_0 be the investment's cash flow if $1 + r_m = 0$

C_f be the cash flow if the market earns r_f.

b be the slope of the cash flow line where $b = \frac{C_f - C_0}{1+r_f}$

*Adapted from Fischer Black, "A Simple Discounting Rule," *Financial Management,* Summer 1988, pp. 7–11.

A One Period Example

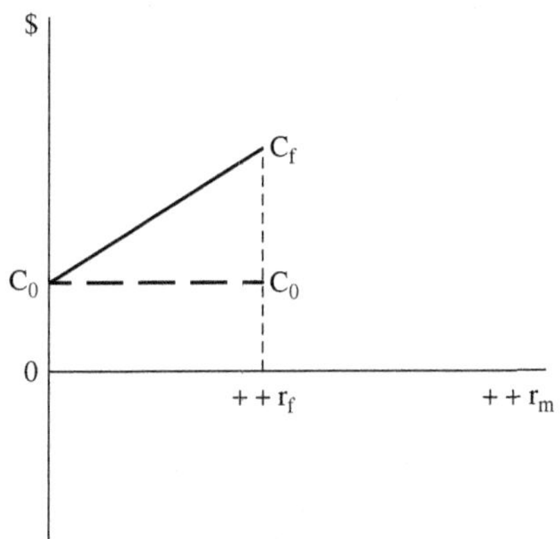

Cash Flow As A Function of $(1 + r_m)$

Assume the cash flow at time one is:

$$X = C_0 + \left(\frac{C_f - C_0}{1 + r_f}\right)(1 + r_m)$$

The present value is:

$$PV = \frac{C_0}{1 + r_f} + \frac{C_f - C_0}{1 + r_f}\left(\frac{1 + r_m}{1 + r_m}\right) = \frac{C_f}{1 + r_f}$$

The period can be of any length of time.

C_0 is discounted at the risk free rate (r_f) since C_0 has zero risk (this cash flow component is not correlated with r_m). The risky component $\frac{C_f - C_0}{1+r_f}(1 + r_m)$ is discounted at r_m, the market rate. The PV is $\frac{C_f}{1+r_f}$. The cash flow could be estimated assuming the market earns a return of r_f, and this cash flow is then discounted at r_f. The cash flow estimate and the discount rate are linked together. The primary problem is that if X is not related in a linear fashion to r_m the simple relationship does not hold.

Multi-Period Example

Let us assume that we want to value a cash flow at time n. Based on the above analysis the value at time (n − 1) is

$$\frac{C_f}{1 + r_f}$$

and since this value is a certainty equivalent the value at time zero is

$$\frac{C_f}{(1 + r_f)^n}.$$

The Power of Compound Interest

The next example is aimed at illustrating the power of compound interest. Assume a paper is folded in half 50 times. The paper is $\frac{1}{450''}$ thick. How "thick" would the fold be?

Answer:

$\frac{1}{12}$ converts to feet

$\frac{1}{5280}$ converts to miles

2^{50} represents the folding in half 50 times

$$\frac{1}{450}\left(\frac{1}{12}\right)\left(\frac{1}{5280}\right)2^{50} = 39{,}500{,}000 \text{ miles}$$

Conclusions

There are two major errors in evaluating investments:

1. Do not have any faith in any calculations, and go "by the seat of the pants".
2. Make all decisions based on the "Accept or Reject" quantitative investment criteria with no qualitative considerations.

Bad capital budgeting techniques are a major handicap likely to prevent the achievement of corporate goals. Not undertaking good projects adds to the risk of a corporation.

Good capital budgeting techniques will enhance managerial capability; they are not a substitute for good management. Calculations are important, but consider the following:

> "The real challenge is creativity and invention, not analysis. Timely execution of projects by entrepreneurial managers is also more critical than sophistication of analytical budgeting techniques." — A Vice President, Finance

Corporate practice has moved from the use of measures (payback and return on investment) that failed to consider effectively time value to an acceptance of discounted cash flow measure. While the cost of capital has been recommended as the discount rate or the hurdle rate to be used by firms, and was used by a large number of firms, the measure implicitly incorporated both time value and risk considerations, and the compound interest calculation using the weighted average cost of capital did not result in a reliable value measure.

A default free time value factor followed logically from the conclusion that risk did not necessarily compound through time. However, this left risk considerations out of the analysis. Sensitivity analysis and simulation, while giving useful insights, did not lead to explicit accept or reject recommendations. Finally, the capital asset pricing model was offered as a possible solution to the problem of how to include time value and risk. Unfortunately, the calculations require unrealistic assumptions and the model is not apt to apply to the specific investment of the firm being analyzed.

Despite the limitations of the capital asset pricing model, business managers should be knowledgeable of its characteristics. It offers a way of quantifying and incorporating risk considerations if the facts of the situation fit. Investments rejected under conventional analysis using the cost of capital might become acceptable, and investments previously considered to be acceptable might be rejected because of their "systematic" risk; that is, the risk that they will go down in value if the general market conditions deteriorate.

Too frequently managers have been unnecessarily confused about the basic nature of the net present value and the internal rate of return methods, thus reluctant to use them. The DCF calculations are powerful tools for evaluating investments. While the uncertainty questions occupy the academic literature, the operating business person should realize that the basic DCF calculations are still the most reliable ways of evaluating investments, and are an important tool in deciding whether or not an investment is acceptable. While we do not have exact decision rules when there is uncertainty, there are known methods of analysis that are useful in coping with investment decision making under uncertainty.

Lecture 33

Three Corporate Finance Issues

A talk given at Homecoming, November 1993, the Johnson Graduate School of Management.

Setting the Stage

Relevant tax law changes

Three Issues

1. Capital structure decisions
2. Dividend policy decisions
3. Mission impossible: Measuring performance

Relevant Tax Law Changes

1. Maximum individual ordinary rate goes from .31 to .396 or higher (other tax provisions).
2. Corporate rate goes from .34 to .35.
3. Capital gains rate stays at .28. Disadvantage of ordinary income:

$$\frac{.31}{.28} - 1 = .107 \qquad \frac{.396}{.28} - 1 = .414$$

4. Small business capital gains (50% exclusion if held for 5 years).

Issue 1: Capital Structure

Assume no investor taxes.

Let t be the corporate tax rate.

It can be shown that:

Value of Levered Firm = Value of Unlevered Firm + t (New Debt) or

$$V_L = V_u + tB$$

and

$$\text{Maximum Value Added} = \frac{t}{1-t} V_u$$

$$\text{If } t = .35 \text{ then } \frac{.35}{1-.35} = .538$$

$$\text{Maximum Value Added} = .538\ V_u \text{ and } V_L = 1.538\ V_u.$$

Conclusion: Value can be increased by a maximum of .538 if assumptions are valid. Other changes can increase value more.

Debt is more attractive than when t = .34.

Example: t = .35, No growth, Cost of capital = .20.

Earnings before interest and taxes = \$200,000

Earnings after taxes with equity = (1 − .35)200,000 = \$130,000

The Unlevered Firm has a value of:

$$V_u = \frac{130,000}{.20} = \$650,000$$

Now substitute \$800,000 of .15 debt for common stock (note \$800,000 is larger than \$650,000).

Interest = .15(800,000) = \$120,000

The investors now earn:

Stock $(200,000 - 120,000)(1 - .35) =$	\$ 52,000
Debt	120,000
Total earnings	\$172,000

$$V_L = V_u + tB = 650,000 + .35(800,000)$$
$$= 650,000 + 280,000 = \$930,000$$

Compare \$930,000 and \$650,000 (values)
\$172,000 and \$130,000 (earnings)

A special strategy

Buy all the stock and (1 − t) of the new debt.

The investor earns \$130,000 with all equity firm.

The investor earns with the \$800,000 debt firm:

Stock investment earns	\$52,000
Debt earns (1 − .35)120,000	78,000
	\$130,000

The earnings are identical.

Conclusion:

There is an investment strategy that will cause the return from a highly levered firm to be identical to the return from an all equity firm.

Note:

There are costs of financial distress.

Adding value to a firm with an initial value of \$650,000

1. Issue \$800,000 of debt paying .15.
2. Pay the \$800,000 from the debt to stockholders.
3. Investor buys (1 − .35)(800,000) of debt = \$520,000

Investment in debt	\$520,000
Common Stock Investment	130,000
Free Value	280,000
New Value for Investor	\$930,000

Would you rather have \$650,000 or \$930,000?

Can also add real value from real changes.
Issue \$1,000,000 of debt (initial value is \$650,000):

$$V_L = V_u + tB = 650,000 + 350,000 = \$1,000,000$$

$$\text{Maximum Value Added} = \frac{350,000}{650,000} = .538.$$

Note: Must be able to use tax deductions.
Must be able to pay interest.

Can buy all \$800,000 of the debt and all the stock (receive \$172,000 rather than \$130,000 per year).

Appendix

Financial strategy: The use of debt symbols to be used

V_u	value of unlevered firm
V_L	value of levered firm
t	corporate tax rate
X	earnings before taxes and before new interest
S	value of stock after issuance of debt
B	value of debt issued
I	interest on new debt issued
$(1 - t)$	fraction of new debt purchased

We want to show that

$$V_L = V_u + tB$$

We will only assume that a given cash flow stream has a given value.

tB is the value added by substituting debt for equity.

Financial Strategy: The Use of Debt

Delevering with taxes

<u>With No New Debt</u>

Buy the stock of firm (V_u)

Investment of V_u
Earn: $(1 - t)X$

With New Debt

Buy same percentage of stock and $(1 - t)$ of debt:

S of stock and earn	$(1 - t)(X - I)$
$(1 - t)B$ of debt and earn	$(1 - t)I$
Sum =	$(1 - t)X$

The same return is earned and the cost (investment) must be the same as the unlevered firm.

With equal investments:

$$V_u = S + (1 - t)B$$

Since $V_L = S + B$:

$$V_u + tB = (S + B) = V_L$$

and

$$V_L = V_u + tB$$

Issue 2: Dividend Policy

Alternatives:

1. Retention
2. Cash dividend
3. DRIP
4. Share repurchase

An Example:

Consider Corporation A with S = \$1,000. $t_p = .396$, $t_g = .28$. Stock Tax Basis = \$1,000

	Investor	Corporation A
Retention	\$ 1,000 of stock	\$1,000 of cash
Cash dividend	\$ 604 of cash	zero cash
DRIP	\$ 1,000 of stock	\$1,000 of cash
	−\$ 396 of cash	
Share repurchase	\$ 1,000 of cash*	zero cash

*With a zero tax basis, the cash would be \$720.

Share repurchase

1. $t_p = .396$, $t_g = .28$. Differential. Tax basis protection.
2. Stock price effects (100,000 shares outstanding)

Value before "dividend"	\$5,000,000	\$50 per share
Dividend	1,000,000	
Value after dividend	\$4,000,000	\$40 per share

With repurchase of 20,000 shares (Price = \$50):

$$\frac{\$4,000,000}{80,000} = \$50.$$

3. Cosmetics.
4. Optional dividend (transaction costs, taxes).
5. Stock options.

Example: $t_p = .396$, $t_g = .28$, Price = \$50

Investor has 100 shares

		Share Repurchase (20 Shares)	
	Dividend = \$10	Tax Basis \$50	Tax Basis \$0
Cash received	\$1,000	\$1,000	\$1,000
Tax	396	0	280
Net	\$ 604	\$1,000	\$ 720

With debt, the firm would have $\frac{\$1,000}{1-.35} = \$1,538.46$:

	Investor Tax Rate $t_P = 0$	Investor Tax Rate $t_p = .396$
Cash	1,538.46	1,538.46
Tax	0	609.23
Net	$1,538.46	$ 929.23

With retention, firm has $1,000 of value.

Issue 3: Measuring Managerial Performance

Some alternatives

Quantitative Measures of "Profits"

a. Operating Margins
   Percentages
   Dollar Amounts
b. ROI or ROE or ROA
c. Economic Income (residual income)
d. Earnings per share (for a period of years)
e. Stockholder Returns (market inputs)

Other considerations:

a. Present growth and foundation for future growth
b. Qualitative factors
c. Other goals and measures (sales, share of market, risk)

Conclusion

We cannot measure managerial performance, but must do so anyway.

ROE, ROI, ROA, Operating Margins, CFROGI all have major deficiencies, but can contribute to an impression.

The best single financial measure is
Economic Income (residual income)

Economic Income

Definition

Income after tax after depreciation after an interest cost of all capital used.

Advantages

a. Any investment with a positive Net Present Value or an Internal Rate of Return larger than the required return will have economic incomes with the same net present value.
b. Will tend to not affect adversely investment or divestment decisions.
c. Management is charged for the capital it uses.

Complexities

a. A year's income may be unsatisfactory, but the investment desirable.
b. Risk differentials (different lived assets).
c. Changing interest rates.

Example: Economic income the firm has a .10 cost of money

Time	Expected Cash Flows
0	−3,000
1	+1,500
2	+1,300
3	+1,200

Economic Incomes:

	Year 1	Year 2	Year 3
Revenues	1,500	1,300	1,200
Depreciation	1,000	1,000	1,000
Income	500	300	200
Interest	300	200	100
Economic Income	200	100	100

Example: Economic income the firm has a .10 cost of money

$$\text{NPV} = -3,000 + \frac{1,500}{1.10} + \frac{1,300}{1.21} + \frac{1,200}{1.331} = \$339.59$$

$$\text{PV of Economic Income} = \frac{200}{1.10} + \frac{100}{1.21} + \frac{100}{1.331} = \$339.59$$

What happens if the firm invests in a project earning less than .10? More than .10?

What happens if the firm earns more than $1,300 in year one?

One Remaining Problem

What happens if cash flows start out relatively slowly?

Needed: A better method of measuring investment and income and depreciation expense.

Solution: Present value depreciation.

Lecture 34

Corporate Finance (1998)

This is a summary of the state of corporate finance.
I do not know to whom or where the talk was given.

Corporate Finance: The Past, Present, and the Future

I will briefly review the history of the academic discipline of finance as well as the contributions of finance practice, and then forecast some changes that will occur in the future.

Corporate finance received a major thrust 43 years ago. In 1951 two books were published that opened the door to new managerial techniques for making capital budgeting decisions using discounted cash flow methods of evaluating investments. *Capital Budgeting* was written by Joel Dean and *The Theory of Investment of the Firm* by Vera and Friedrich Lutz.

Dean, a respected academician who did a large amount of business consulting, wrote his book for business teachers and managers. The Lutzes were economists interested in capital theory, and wrote their book for the economic academic community. Both books were extremely well written and are understandable. They initially caused academics and subsequently business managers to rethink how capital investments should be reevaluated. Up to the late 1950's payback and accounting return on investment were the two primary capital budgeting methods used by large firms, with less than 5% of the largest firms using a DCF method.

Today, almost all large corporations use at least one DCF method. Unfortunately, approximately 50% of these firms also still use accounting ROI to evaluate investments. This is unfortunate since ROI is a very flawed technique for evaluating investments.

The second major thrust in corporate finance came in June 1958 when Franco Modigliani and Merton Miller published their classic paper on capital structure in the *American Economic Review.*

The paper proved that the value of a firm was independent of its capital structure, thus the firm's capital structure decision was irrelevant. Fortunately, this faulty conclusion was soon adjusted to the correct position that in the presence of corporate income taxes and financial distress costs, capital structure would affect value. The position was then adjusted to consider the effect of investor taxes on the capital structure decision. Today, there is agreement that capital structure decisions are important, though a clever tax law can decrease their importance.

In 1952 Markowitz published a book and a paper that launched modern portfolio theory. Portfolio theory received additional momentum when in 1964, William Sharpe, building on Harry Markowitz's portfolio theory, derived the Capital Asset Pricing Model (CAPM). This model which directly affects investment strategy also greatly affects corporate finance. It suggests that unsystematic risk is diversified away by investors thus not relevant, but that systematic risk must be considered. Firms do not have to diversify activities to reduce risk, investors can diversify to the extent they desire diversification.

In 1973 there was the fourth major development. Fischer Black and Myron Scholes published a paper in *The Journal of Political Economy* on the pricing of options, and offered a unique method of valuing options. The Black-Scholes valuation formula is already widely used in all financial markets. It is also highly important for many hedging activities and has significant capital budgeting implications that are beginning to be understood. Most importantly, option theory introduces a new way to think about corporate finance and investing.

In the 1980s academic theory development took second place to three real world financial developments. One was the development of the junk bond market and the tremendous implications this market had to corporate finance practices. The second development was the initiation of the swap market and its rapid growth. The third development was the rapid expansion in the market for futures and other derivative securities. The origin of important financial developments is not restricted to the academic community.

Two other developments that merit inclusion are efficient markets theory in the 1950s and 1960s and the subsequent anomalies of the '80 and '90s, and Jensen- Meckling's (1976) introduction of agency theory, and our expanding knowledge of markets (micro-market theory).

Where is finance today and where is it heading?

Let us return to the topic of capital budgeting where today 100% or nearly 100% of the largest industrial firms use one or more DCF methods. The first and easiest step for improvement is for firms to stop using the ROI method for evaluating investments. This method is misleading and supplies no useful information.

The second improvement is more difficult, but also more important. It is not likely to be correct to apply the formula $(1+r)^{-n}$ using one value of r to transform all cash flows of all time periods back to the present, if r includes both a pure time value and a risk factor. Thus we can expect better methods of taking into consideration risk and time value than using a risk adjusted discount rate (r) in the formula $(1+r)^{-n}$. This implies that strategy considerations will strongly affect a firm's allocation of resources rather than have the allocation merely be a mathematical exercise.

The third change is an increase in the application to option theory to capital budgeting decisions and to common stock valuation.

We also need to reconsider the capital structure choice. One has to be careful here since the recommendation has to be location specific. In the United States, with Drexel Burnham driven out of existence, firms no longer have an incentive to design a shareholder value maximizing capital structure. The pressure from corporate raiders is off. Raiders find it difficult to raise capital. It is important to understand what junk bonds (and Drexel Burnham) did and did not do. They did:

a. finance the acquisition of real assets
b. finance acquisitions of firms
c. finance LBO's
d. reduce the income taxes of some restructured firms and increase shareholder value
e. cause uneasiness in many board rooms
f. give investors an interesting choice (high risk — high yield debt).

They did not:

a. increase the risk of any issuing corporation (they did increase the risk of the remaining stock)
b. they did not increase the risk to investors (initial equity investors could subsequently increase or decrease their risk)
c. they did not put economically desirable workers of jobs (economically profitable workers were retained by profit minded investors).
d. they did not decrease social welfare.

Junk bonds are a means of financing, more risky than investment grade debt, but less risky than an equal amount of equity for the same corporation. They deserve careful analysis, not a negative evaluation based on prejudice and emotion.

Today a redesign of the capital structure of the average U.S. firm could increase stockholder value significantly. A change in dividend policy could add more value. Investors seeking increased returns will discover that corporate financial engineering can increase shareholders' value and that there will be moves to exploit these opportunities.

Ultimately, governments will become aware that all capital sources are equivalent (back to M-M, 1958) and should be taxed on an equivalent (equal handed) manner. It might take longer for the U.S. Government to take action, but someday, even a U.S. corporation will not be able to find a tax advantage in financial engineering. That is not the situation today. There is money to be made.

My next forecast has to do with the growth of the derivative market associated with hedging operations. One forecast in this area is that firms will switch from each operating unit doing its own hedging to hedging from a corporate world-wide perspective. Secondly, firms will reconsider the cost-benefits of hedging. Who benefits from costly hedging operations? There will not be a disappearance of hedging, but rather more of a willingness for a corporation to accept a reasonable level of risk. We all have life insurance when we have small children and we tend to insure our homes against fire and other disasters. But there are other risks of loss that we are willing to accept and do not insure. In like manner, corporations do not need to hedge all hedgeable risks.

My next forecast has to do with corporate ownership and governance. I expect shareholders to increase their activity in controlling the activities of business. This applies to institutional investors, but also to a second group of shareholders. We will see more corporations controlled by their managers and workers through significant stock ownership.

In the future we can expect there to be relatively more significant changes in financial strategy than changes in financial securities. In the past 20 years innovations in financial securities have been driven by:

a. tax considerations
b. governmental regulations
c. advent of powerful and accessible computers
d. increase in foreign trade and international finance transactions
e. increase in the knowledge of persons working in finance.

Even if we do not expect the influence of taxation, regulation, computers, and the knowledge of participants to grow significantly, there is reason to expect that there will be a large number of significant security innovations linked to the computational capability of computers and to an increase in the volume of foreign currency transactions. The opportunities for improved financial strategies and the opportunities for financial innovations remain large.

In addition, an expansion in the separation of internal and external reporting, would be desirable. It is not appropriate that internal reporting be restricted to the standards of GAAP.

There is one final forecast, which is the most important and the safest of all forecasts. Future events will be different than those forecasted by me or by anyone else. The only way to cope with the future is to have a fundamental understanding of good corporate decision-making and analyze, using good theory, the new economic environment when it arrives.

Future finance experts will be concerned with the same types of problems as we are. There will never be a capital budgeting method that insures that the cash flow inputs are perfectly correct. There will never be a capital structure model that allows us to perfectly balance the tax and other advantages of one capital structure with the costs of financial distress. There are few, if any, perfect financial hedges. There are many things we do not know, and objectives we do not know how to achieve.

These are the best of times, except for those of the future, and together we can improve the future.

Lecture 35

Investing in an Uncertain World

Investment advice given in August 2000.

Question: In what year would you earn the highest annual return (54%) by investing in stocks?

History

For any 20 year holding period the common stock return is positive.

Long-term bonds beat common stock for the three 20 year holding periods:

1928 to 47
1929 to 48
1930 to 49

Is history a good predictor of the future?

Some Useful Insights

1. The old adage "Buy Low, Sell High" is not operational. What is low? What is high? Sell a stock if you need cash, need to diversify, need a tax loss, or your tax situation has changed. "Buy Low" is good advice (but not operational). "Realize your gains" merely increases taxes and transaction costs.

2. Never act on advice (a tip) that leads to buying without your checking on the facts. A tip is information that is too good to be true, and likely is.
   Do some basic financial analysis to convince yourself fundamental value lies behind a purchase. If you are risk averse, you might listen to a sell tip. The key to this rule is risk aversion.
3. The "Greater Fool Theory" is an unreliable basis for betting one's wealth.
4. "Dollar averaging" is a good procedure for ensuring that you do not hoard cash when stock prices are lower than they used to be. It does not increase your expected return. Increases risk (no diversification).

First Purchase	100 @ $40	= 4,000
Second Purchase	200 @ $20	= 4,000
	300@ $26.67	8,000

   You can lower average cost more by doubling investment.
5. Preferred stock is not a good investment for a high tax or a low tax investor (OK to consider preferred stock if you are a corporation). Does not apply to deep discount (high yield) or convertible preferred.
6. Do not expect to find experts or decision rules that tell you the direction of the next move of the market or of a stock. Market turns are predictable only after the fact!
7. Stop losses give you the opportunity to avoid an upturn.

Conclusions

1. Diversify.
2. Taxes (institutional factors) are relevant.
3. Markets are relatively efficient.
4. Basic analysis is useful.
5. Do not rely on someone dumber than you to bail you out.
6. Beware "rules of thumb" without theory: many things we "know" are not so.
7. Market turns are difficult to predict (the future is uncertain).

8. There are risk and return trade-offs.
9. All stock market crashes are predicted. More are predicted than occur.
10. Not all crashes are harmful for very long. The difficulty is buying at the bottom of the crash.

> *"I have reluctantly reached the conclusion that nothing is more suicidal than a rational investment policy in an irrational world."*
>
> *John Maynard Keynes*

Lecture 36

My Best MBA Lecture

The date and location of this lecture is not known. I guess 2000.

My Best MBA Lecture (Not the most important)

A Brief History of Modern Finance

1. 1951, Two Books:
   Capital Budgeting (Joel Dean)
   The Theory of Investment (Vera and Friedrich Lutz)
2. June 1958, Franco Modigliani and Merton Miller
   American Economic Review, "The Cost of Capital..."
   Capital Structure
3. 1957, Harry Markowitz
   Book: *Portfolio Selection*
4. 1964, William Sharpe (also Lintner, Tobin, Merton)
   The Journal of Finance
   CAPM "Capital Asset Prices..."
5. 1973, Fischer Black and Myron Scholes
   The Journal of Political Economy, "The Pricing of Options..."

REAL WORLD (1980–2000)

1. Junk bonds
2. Swap market
3. Futures market for financial securities
4. Options and other derivatives

Junk Bonds

Used to:

a. Finance the acquisition of real assets.
b. Finance acquisition of firms.
c. Finance LBOs.
d. Reduce the income taxes of some restructured firms and increase shareholder value.
e. Cause uneasiness in many board rooms.
f. Give investors an interesting choice (high risk and high yield debt).

They did not:

a. Increase the risk of any issuing corporation (they did increase the risk of the remaining stock).
b. Increase the risk to investors (initial equity investors could subsequently increase or decrease their risk).
c. Put economically desirable workers out of work (economically profitable workers were retained by profit minded investors).
d. Decrease social welfare.

Taxes and Financial Strategy

Tax Rates: $t_p = .396$, $t_g = .20$

$$\frac{.396}{.200} - 1 = .98$$

Also, tax deferral.

Assume Corporation earns .1658 after tax.

Investors earn $.1658(1 - .396) = .100$

<u>Retention</u> $(n = .10)$

$$1(1.1656)^{10}(1 - .20) = \$3.70$$

<u>Dividend</u> $1(1 - .396)(1.10)^{10} = \$1.57$

It makes a difference.

Lecture 37

Ten Ways

This talk was given in 2000. I do not know to whom this was given. The recommendations are sensible.

Ten Ways to Increase Stockholder Value with Finance

1. Tax laws affect the use of different types of capital. Use this information.
   For example, Japan's not taxing capital gains motivated zero coupon bonds in the United States.
   For example, in the United States, debt has an edge.
2. Retained earnings versus dividends or share repurchase.
   Dividends versus DRIP.
   Stock repurchase versus dividends.
   Conclusion: Define a corporate financial personality.
3. Pension payment timing is important (a tax arbitrage possibility).
4. Buy versus lease analysis must be done properly. Leasing may be incorrectly encouraged.
5. Credit granting decisions are "marginal" decisions deserving of correct economic analysis.
6. Make "correct" capital budgeting (efficiency and expansion) decisions. Cost of retained earnings versus cost of new capital.
7. Mergers and Acquisitions, LBOs, and MBOs. What are the sources of gains?

8. Performance measurement and the managerial incentive system.
9. Divestments. When are they desirable?
10. Control speculation and hedging.

Conclusions

a. Financial decisions depend on where the corporation is on the globe.
b. Good finance is important if the firm wants to maximize stockholder value.

Lecture 38

Investment Strategies in an Uncertain World

This lecture was given in 2003. Where is unknown.

"It is not easy to get rich in Las Vegas, at Churchill Downs, or at the local Merrill Lynch office." — Paul A. Samuelson, "Mathematics of Speculative Price," p. 5 in *SIAM*, January 1973.

In the words of one expert: "When you have a feel for the market, you are probably catching cold."

Stocks are Risky

1929

Dow Jones hit September High of 386

Monday, October 21: Dow Jones 321 (Close)

Thursday, October 24: Dow Jones 272 (Low for day)

Tuesday, October 29: Dow Jones 212 (Low for day)

Month's High: 359

$$\frac{147}{359} = 41\% \text{ drop over month (high to low)}$$

1987

August 25, 1987: Dow Jones <u>2722</u> (High)

$$\frac{983}{2{,}722} = 36\% \text{ Drop over two months}$$

October 19, 1987:

$$\frac{508}{2{,}246} = 23\% \text{ Single Day Drop}$$

History

For a 20 year holding period the common stock return is positive.

Long-term bonds beat common stock for the three 20 year holding periods:

1928 to 47
1929 to 48
1930 to 49

Is history a good predictor of the future?

Assume there is extra cash

The alternatives are:

a. Mutual funds

<u>Advantages:</u>

Diversification
Expert management
Ease

<u>Disadvantages:</u>

Cost
Turnover: Realization of taxable capital gains.

b. Common stock
c. Preferred stock (competing with corporate buyers)
d. Special Preferreds — PERCS

e. Debt
   Corporate (AAA to BB)
   Tax Exempts
   Treasuries (Bills to 30 year Strips)
   CD's
f. Exotic alternatives:
   Vacation home(s) Art, stamps, coins Cornell University

Tax strategies

Preferred stock (e.g. PERCS), high dividend common, and debt should be in tax protected vehicles. Capital gain common stock can be held outside of tax protected vehicles.

Tax strategies include:

a. SRA, IRA, Keogh Plan, 40lK, etc.
b. Tax exempt bonds
c. Gifts to children (spread income).
d. Some non-dividend paying common stocks
e. Buy real assets (stamps, art, coins, land, gems, etc.). Distinquish between gambling and investing.
f. Buy and manage real estate (ugh!).
g. Tax sheltered earnings (options, deferred pay).

Common Stocks

Three issues:

a. Extent of diversification.
b. Which stock?
c. What allocation?

Diversification

Consider the following table showing "Risk Reduction".

With 10 securities you reduce 90% of the risk that can be reduced!

With 100 securities you reduce 99% of the risk that can be reduced.

However, you reduce more risk if the securities have a relatively low correlation (connection).

Risk Reduction: Portfolio Variance as Fraction of Individual Security Variance

Number of Securities in the Portfolio	Correlation between Securities (r)					Percent of Max Risk Reduction
	1.0	0.8	.05	0.1	0	N-1/N
2	1.0	0.9	0.75	0.55	0.50	1/2
10	1.0	0.82	0.55	0.19	0.10	9/10
100	1.0	0.802	0.505	0.109	0.01	99/100
∞	1.0	0.800	0.500	0.100	0.00	1

When can risk be reduced to zero?

The stock market throughout history has been a "fair gamble" and you should always own some stock. The casino in Ledyard offers "unfair" gambles.

Which Stock?

What company should you invest in?

a. Do you know a good person heading a corporation you would like to invest in?
b. Do you know a product that is so good you want to invest in the firm?
c. Do you know a firm whose style (concept) you like?

What industry? What firm in that industry?

a. Use your special (not inside) information.
b. Diversify

Note: There can be a good firm with a good product, but it is a bad common stock investment (the stock price is too high) or the firm has "bad luck".

Conclusion: Diversify.

The Allocation

The allocation between stock and other investments, including cash.

We know that for any 30 year time period since 1926, you are better off holding common stock than other security.

However, there are some (20) years in which the return from holding common stock is negative and additional years when stock did not do as well as debt.

We know that we cannot pick the moment of maximum stock market level nor determine when the market has reached a bottom.

We are not good allocating investments.

However, based on past history one should be 100% in stock if you believe history repeats itself, and you will hold the investment for at least 30 years after the worst market collapse.

With less certain beliefs, you should not have 100% of your savings in stocks.

Does history repeat itself?

Strategies That Can Lead to Maximum Returns (and Maximum Losses)

1. Buy one "best" stock.
2. Buy one "best" call option.
3. Buy stock market index futures.
4. Use debt to do any of the above.
5. Some investment funds use preferred stock for leverage.
6. Sell "puts" (and have stocks go up).
7. Own no stocks (and have stocks go down and stay down).

You have to ask the right questions. Moses Malone[1] was asked: "*What is the difference between 42 points Tuesday and 12 points Thursday?*" Moses replied, 30 points.

[1] An American basketball player.

After he had been retired for thirty years Carl Hubbell[2] was asked how he thought he could pitch against modern baseball teams. He replied: "*My god, I've got spurs and calcium deposits and everything else. I couldn't throw a ball from here to the end of the table.*"

Common Stock Dividends and Capital Gains

Assume:

Capital gains tax rate = .20
Ordinary income tax rate = .396
Return (after tax) investors can earn = .0604
Return corporation can earn = .10
Investment horizon = 15 years
Corporation has $100 that it can invest or pay a dividend.

Dividend

Investor nets $60.40:

$$60.40(1.0604)^{15} = \$145.57$$

Retention and then Capital Gain

$$100(1.1)^{15}(1 - .20) = \$334.18$$

Bonds versus Stock

The bond "P/E"

We can compute the contractual yield from investing in a bond (the actual may differ because of financial distress or early call).

Assume a bond contractual yield is .08.

A measure comparable to a P/E is obtained by dividing 1 by .08:

$$\text{"P/E"} = \frac{1}{.08} = 12.5$$

A $1,000 bond pays $80 interest.

The bond is selling at 12.5 times interest.

[2] An American baseball player.

The P/E for stock

A stock has three relevant measures:

1. Dividends
2. Earnings
3. Cash flow from operations (after maintenance capital expenditures)

Assume a stock selling for \$100 has:

$$\text{Dividends} = \$1,\ \text{Earnings} = \$4,\ \text{Cash flow} = \$10$$

The <u>P/E</u> is:

$$\text{P/E} = \frac{100}{4} = 25$$

The <u>Cash Flow Multiplier</u> is

$$\text{Cash Flow Multiplier} = \frac{100}{10} = 10 \text{ times}$$

The <u>Dividend Multiplier</u> is:

$$\text{Dividend Multiplier} = \frac{100}{1} = 100 \text{ times}$$

Stocks or Bonds ($k_e < k_i$) Invest \$1,000: Future Value

<u>Debt ($k_i = .06$)</u>

$$\begin{aligned}\text{Future Value} &= 39\ \text{B}(20, .039)(1.039)^{20} + 1,000\\ &= 1,149 + 1,000 = \$2,149\end{aligned}$$

or

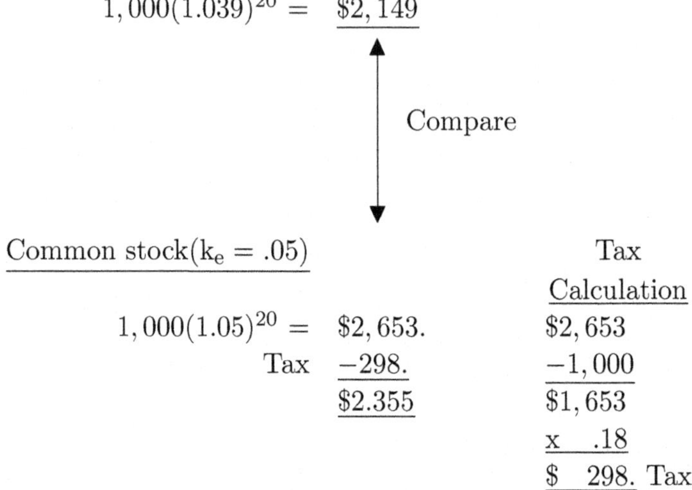

Some Useful Insights

1. The old adage "Buy Low, Sell High" is wrong. Never sell a stock voluntarily unless you need cash, a tax loss, or your tax situation has changed. "Buy Low" is good advice (but not operational). "Realize your gains" merely increases taxes and transaction costs.
2. Never act on advice (a tip) that leads to buying without your checking on the facts. A tip is information that is too good to be true, and likely is.
   Do some basic financial analysis to convince yourself fundamental value lies behind a purchase. If you are risk adverse, you might listen to a sell tip. The key to this rule is risk aversion.
3. The "Greater Fool Theory" is an unreliable basis for betting one's wealth.
4. "Dollar averaging" is a good procedure for ensuring that you do not hoard cash when stock prices are lower than they used to be. It does not increase your expected return. Increases risk (no diversification).

First Purchase	100 @ \$40	= 4,000
Second Purchase	200 @ \$20	= 4,000
	300@ \$26.67	8,000

You can lower average cost more by doubling investment.

5. Preferred stock is not a good investment for a high tax or a low tax investor (OK to consider preferred stock if you are a corporation). Does not apply to deep discount (high yield) or convertible preferred.
6. Do not expect to find experts or decision rules that tell you the direction of the next move of the market or of a stock. Market turns are predictable only after the fact!
7. Stop losses give you the opportunity to avoid an upturn.

Conclusions

1. Diversify
2. Taxes (institutional factors) are relevant.
3. Markets are relatively efficient.
4. Basic analysis is useful.
5. Do not rely on someone dumber than you to bail you out.
6. Beware "rules of thumb" without theory; many things we "know" are not so.
7. Market turns are difficult to predict (the future is uncertain).
8. There are risk and return trade-offs.
9. All stock market crashes are predicted. More are predicted than occur.
10. Not all crashes are harmful for very long. The difficulty is buying at the bottom of the crash.

"I have reluctantly reached the conclusion that nothing is more suicidal than a rational investment policy in an irrational world."

John Maynard Keynes

Lecture 39

Chicago Talk to Alumni

This talk compared 1929 to the present (March 2009).

Comparing 1929 and 2008–2009

Things that are the same and different.

<u>The Same</u>

> Irving Fisher in November 1929: "...stocks will soon recover a considerable part of lost ground" and "business prospects are excellent." He bought stocks in November, 1929 with borrowed funds.
>
> *Forbes*, (Nov. 15, 1929), p. 24.

Hal Bierman in November, 2008: "Buy"

1929

> Senator Glass: "Mr. Whitney, right on that point may I ask you a question: What percentage of the public is [sic] speculating in stocks of the stock exchange understand the real intrinsic value of the stocks in which they deal?"
>
> 1931 — Hearings before the U.S. Senate Committee on Banking and Currency on stock exchange practices.

> "One of these clouds was an American wave of optimism, born of continued progress over the decade, which the Federal Reserve Board transformed into the stockexchange Mississippi Bubble."
>
> Herbert Hoover, *The Memoirs of Herbert Hoover* (New York: Macmillan, 1952), p. 5.

"We attempt to Stop the Orgy of Speculation."

Title of Chapter 2, *The Memoirs of Herbert Hoover*

The *Federal Reserve Bulletin* of February 1929 made it clear that the federal reserve banks would take steps to decrease the flow of credit to "speculators". The bulletin stated that the Fed "means to restrain the use, either directly or indirectly, of federal reserve credit facilities in aid of the growth of speculative credit."

In 1929, the enemy were speculators:

> Senator Glass: "It was selling at 108 in January. It was selling on the market yesterday at 69. Now, what is that but gambling?"
>
> Senate Committee on Banking and Currency (1928), p. 80.

	Market Value (All listed stocks)		**A Fall of**
September 1, 1929	$89.7 billion	100%	0%
November 1, 1929	71.8	80%	20%
July 1, 1932	15.6	17%	83%

"On the first of January of 1929, as a matter of probability, it was most likely that the boom would end before the year was out."

J.K. Galbraith, *The Great Crash, 1929* (pp. 16, 29)

"Playing as I often do the experiment of studying price profiles with their dates concealed, I discovered that I would have been caught by the 1929 debacle."

P.A. Samuelson, *Journal of Portfolio Management*, Fall 1979, p. 9.

"The collapse from 1929 to 1933 was neither foreseeable nor inevitable."

M. Friedman and A.J. Schwartz, *A Monetary History of the United States*, 1867–1960, p. 247.

October 1929

Dow Jones

October 1929 359 High

October 1929 212 Low (Low for day, Black Thursday)

A 41% drop

2008

> "Who wanted to hear from dismal economists warning that the whole thing was, in effect, a giant Ponzi scheme."
>
> Paul Krugman, *NY Times*, November 28, 2008, p. A43.

> "This woman wasn't saying that Wall Street bankers were corrupt. She was saying they were stupid."
>
> Thomas Friedman quoting Michael Lewis quoting Meredith Whitney, *NY Times*, November 21, 2008.

What is Needed

— Broad rules and regulation on an international basis.

— Control amount of debt given the amount of risk and equity.

Debt and Risk

No Debt

$$\mathrm{Var(r)} = \mathrm{Var}\left(\frac{\mathrm{X}}{\mathrm{S}}\right) = \frac{1}{\mathrm{S}^2}\mathrm{Var\ X}$$

Define Var X to be the firm's risk
Var (r) to be the variance of the stockholder return on investment

Debt of B

$$\mathrm{Var(r)} = \mathrm{Var}\frac{\mathrm{X-I}}{\mathrm{S-B}} = \left(\frac{1}{\mathrm{S-B}}\right)^2 \mathrm{VarX}$$

Example

<u>No Debt</u>

Let Var $X = 100$

$S = 10$ Firm size

$$\text{Var(r)} = \frac{1}{100}(100) = 1$$

<u>Debt</u>

Debt = \$9

Stock = 1

$$\text{Var(r)} = \left(\frac{1}{10-9}\right)^2 \text{Var X} = 100 \text{ (compare with 1)}$$

Now: 100 times more risk

Debt/Stock = 30

Assume

$$30S_0 = B$$

and

$$S_0 + B = 10$$
$$31S_0 = 10$$
$$S_0 = .32258 \quad B = 9.6774$$
$$\text{Var(r)} = \left(\frac{1}{.32258}\right) \text{VarX} = (3.10)^2 \text{VarX}$$

Var(r) = 9.61(100) = 961 Compared to 1 with zero debt and 100 with \$9 debt.

Lecture 40

Increasing Shareholder Value: A Financial Strategies Presentation

This is near the end of the lecture series and summarizes the current state of knowledge. I do not know the immediate purpose of this lecture.

Objective of Lecture

Communicate the hypothesis that financial strategies can significantly affect shareholder value.

> "Ezra Cornell acquired a fortune, as one may say, by misadventure, by violating all the rules of prudence and common sense and adhering, with stubborn tenacity, contrary to experience and all sound advice, to a settled conviction."
>
> Carl L. Becker
> Cornell University (1943)

Two Fundamental Questions

How does a firm make profits?

a. Clever sales and marketing (prices, distribution, etc.)
b. Technological break-through in product or production (including out-sourcing)

c. Management and organization (lower costs, purchasing, etc.)
d. Expand markets
e. Design or delivery of products
f. Have a monopoly (or near monopoly)
g. A fortuitous event (find oil, etc.)

How does one increase the value of a firm through finance?

a. Capital budgeting
b. Capital structure
c. Dividend policy
d. Other

Financial Strategies

Three types of financial strategies

1. Real (affect assets and liabilities independent of institutional factors).
2. Motivated by institutional factors (e.g., taxes and regulations).
3. Magic.

Type 1: Real

a. Correct evaluation of real investments (capital budgeting). The discount rate. Options. Risk.
b. Buy versus lease decisions.
c. Congruent performance measurement and good investment policies.
d. Mergers and acquisitions.
e. Working capital decisions (inventories, credit, etc.).
f. Risk management.

Each topic deserves expansion.

Type 2: Motivated by institutional factors

a. Substitution of debt for equity (capital structure).
b. Substitution of retention for dividends.
c. Utilization of share repurchase.
d. Mergers and acquisitions (this is also "real").

The above can be "dressed up" by using convertibles, zeros, etc., but tax considerations normally generate the value.

These strategies are most important for firms with incomes.

Type 3: Magic

These strategies rely on someone being fooled (a greater fool theory of finance).

a. Letter, target, or tracking stock.
b. Dividend reinvestment plans compared to retained earnings. A growth company paying increasing dividends.
c. A high P/E firm acquiring a low P/E firm.
d. Decisions for accounting effects (operating leases are off the balance sheet).
e. Stock dividends and stock splits.
f. Hedging a share repurchase program.

The Limits of Value from Capital Structure

With no costs of financial distress it can be shown that:

$$\mathrm{V_L} = \mathrm{V_u} + tB$$

where

$\mathrm{V_L}$ is the value of the levered firm
$\mathrm{V_u}$ is the value of the unlevered firm

t is the corporate tax rate

B is the debt that is added in substitution of common stock equity.

With maximum debt and t = .35, we have

$$V_L = \frac{V_u}{1 - t} = 1.54\,V_u$$

Value can be increased by 54%.

But there are complexities:

a. Investor taxes
b. Costs of financial distress (including an inability of the firm to execute real plans).
c. Stockholders benefit, but CEO incurs the cost. Today there is little or no incentive for a firm to increase the percentages of debt.

Dividend versus Retained Earnings

Investor earns .085 (tax rate is .15).

Corporation earns .10.

A fifteen year horizon.

With a $100 dividend and then investment for 15 years.

$$(1 - .15)100(1.085)^{15} = \$289$$

With retention:

$$100(1.10)^{15} = \$418.$$

With retention and then the capital gains taxed at .15:

$$100(1.10)^{15}(1 - .15) = \$355.$$

Value is increased.

Also, there are the savings of the other fourteen years.

The tax rate on dividends may be larger than .15.

Share Repurchase versus Dividends

Ordinary income tax rate = .36: Dividend tax rate = .15. Capital gains rate = .15

Price = Tax Basis = $20 per share

$100,000 available. 100,000 shares (investor owns 1,000 shares). Market Cap = $2,000,000.

<u>Cash Dividend</u>

Investor receives $\$1 \times 1,000 =$	$1,000
Tax (.15)	– 150
	$ 850

<u>Share Repurchase</u>

Investor sells 50 shares for $20 per share.
Investor receives $50 \times 20 = \underline{\$1,000}$ (no tax, no gain)
Investor does not have to sell.

Stock Price Effect (Initial Price = $20)

Common Stock Value	$2,000,000
less (repurchase)	– 100,000
New Value	$1,900,000

After dividend:

$$\text{P} = \frac{1,900,000}{100,000} = \$19$$

After share repurchase (5,000 shares)

$$\text{P} = \frac{1,900,000}{95,000} = \$20 \text{ (no change)}$$

But through time with Div equal to 5% of market capitalization the price will grow at:

$$g = \frac{\text{Div}}{\text{V} - \text{Div}} = \frac{100,000}{2,000,000 - 100,000} = .0526$$

Assume zero real growth. At time one:

$$P_1 = \frac{2,000,000}{95,000} = \$21.05$$

or equivalently $P_1 = 20(1.0526) = \$21.05$

Stock Price Growth

At time 20, the \$20 stock price will grow to:

$$P_{20} = (1+g)^{20} P_0 = 1.0526^{20}(20) = \$55.76$$

This is with zero real growth. With real growth of .07, we have

$$g = \frac{.07 + .0526}{1 - .0526} = .1294$$

$$P_{20} = (1.1294)^{20}(20) = \$228.$$

Share Repurchase

1. Stock price effect
2. EPS effect (and other cosmetic changes)
3. Firm buys undervalued stock
4. Partial LBO (managerial control)
5. Tax effects for investor (tax deferral, capital gains tax rate, tax basis protection)
6. Optional dividend for investor (save transaction costs)
7. Firm can buy odd lots of its stock
8. Signal to market (stock is undervalued, etc.)
9. Buy shares for corporate use (avoid dilution)
10. Flexible dividend (for firm and for investors)
11. Best use of cash compared to real investments?

Conclusions

a. Financial decisions are affected by institutions (e.g., tax laws) therefore the location of the corporation affects its decisions.

b. Corporate financial decisions are important if the firm wants to maximize shareholder value.
c. Real financial strategies are not subject to national boundaries.
d. To increase a firm's value with finance, a firm must have basic value.

> "Those who compare the age on which their lot has fallen with a golden age which exists only in their imagination may talk of degeneracy and decay: but no man who is correctly informed as to the past will be disposed to take a morose or desponding view of the present."
>
> Thomas Macauley

These are the best of times, except for the future and we can improve the future.

Lecture 41

Financial Strategies

Increasing the value of a firm via corporate finance.

How Does One Increase the Value of a Firm Through Finance?

a. Capital Budgeting
b. Capital structure
c. Dividend policy
d. Other

Capital Budgeting

a. The choice of the discount rate(s).
b. Valuing real options
c. Buy versus lease decisions
d. Performance measurement consistent with good investment policies
e. Risk Management

Capital Structure

With no costs of financial distress it can be shown that:

$$\mathrm{V_L = V_u + tB}$$

where

V_L is the value of the levered firm
V_u is the value of the unlevered firm
t is the corporate tax rate
B is the debt that is added in substitution of common stock equity.

With maximum debt and t = .35 we have

$$V_L = \frac{V_u}{1 - t} = 1.54V_u$$

Value can be increased by 54%.

But there are complexities:

a. Investor taxes
b. Costs of financial distress (including an inability of the firm to execute real plans).
c. Stockholders benefit, but CEO incurs the cost. Today there is little or no incentive for a firm to increase the percentages of debt.
d. Effect of debt issuance on EPS.

Dividend versus Retained Earnings

Investor earns .065 (tax rate is .36).

Corporation earns .10

A fifteen year horizon.

With a $100 dividend and then investment for 15 years.

$$(1 - .36)100(1.064)^{15} = \$162$$

With retention:

$$100(1.10)^{15} = \$418$$

With retention and then a capital gains taxed at .18:

$$100(1.10)^{15}(1 - .18) = \$343$$

Value is more than doubled by retention. Also, there are the savings of the other fourteen years.

Tax "Reform"

Assume dividends are allowed as a deduction by the corporation.

$$t_c = .35, \quad t_p = .36, \quad t_g = .20$$

a. What is better, debt or common stock?
b. What is better, dividends or retained earnings?
c. What is better, dividends or share repurchase?

Dividends as Tax Deduction

Debt or common stock?

	Dept	Common Stock	Retained Earnings
EBIT	$100	$100	$100
Interest or Dividend	100	100	
Corporate Tax	0	0	35
Investor Tax	36	36	
Net	$64	$64	$65*

*There will be a tax to investor when the stock is sold.

Debt is not more desirable than stock.

Dividend or share repurchase?

Consider a share repurchase. There is $35 of corporate tax. The cash flow to investors is $65 but this is taxed ($t_g = .20$).

With more than \$65 of the basis the investor nets more than \$65.

With \$65 of tax basis the investor nets \$65.

With \$0 of tax basis the investor nets .8(65) = \$52.

Dividends give \$64. Inconclusive.

Dividends are Not Taxed (Bush Proposal)

$t_p = .36$ but t_p is reduced to Zero for Dividends

$t_c = .35$

No change in corporate taxes

	Debt	Common Stock (Dividend)	Common Stock (Retention)	Common Stock (Share Repurchase)
EBIT	\$100	\$100	\$100	\$100
Corporate Tax	0	35	35	35
Investor Tax	36	0	0	Some Tax
Net	\$64**	\$65	\$65*	Less than \$65

1. Common stock beats debt for taxed investor
2. Dividend is as good as retention
3. Dividend beats share repurchase for taxed investor

*There is some tax in the future (there is a change in the investor's tax basis).
**Could be \$100

Dividend is Taxed

Assume Tax on Dividends is Reduced to .20.

$t_g = .20$.

	Debt	Common Stock (Dividend)	Common Stock (Retention)	Common Stock (Share Repurchase)
EBIT	$100	$100	$100	$100
Corporate Tax	0	35	35	35
Investor Tax	36	13*	0**	0**
Net	$64	$52	$65	$ 65

*Dividend is $65.
**The tax in the future may be as high as .20 (65) = $13. But this amount must be time discounted.

Dividends are almost as good as other common stock alternatives, but still inferior.

Dividends Not Taxed: Happy or Sad?

Happy

1. Large shareholders in dividend paying stocks in taxable accounts
2. Gov't bond traders (larger U.S. deficit)
3. Investment banks (corporations must raise capital)
4. Bush

Sad

1. Managers who are thoughtful (lose share repurchase as the "obvious" choice)
2. Small or zero shareholders
3. Finance professors
4. Average U.S. citizen
5. Insurance Companies selling annuities or retirement plans
6. Banks

Rankings for Investors (not a forecast)

Before Bush	If Bush Wins
1. Retained Earnings	1. Dividends with DRP
2. Share Repurchase	2. Dividends (100%)
3. a. Dividends	3. Retained Earnings (deemed a dividend)
b. Dividends & DRP	4. Share Repurchase (but still popular with managers).
Conclusions:	**Conclusions:**
a. Most corporations should <u>not</u> pay dividends	a. All corporations should pay 100% of earnings as dividends or a deemed dividend.
b. Managers and shareholders have same strategy.	b. Different for Managers

NOTE: a. Partial repeal of Capital Gains Tax (deemed dividend)
b. A record-keeping mess.

Share Repurchase versus Dividends

Ordinary income tax rate = .36

Capital gains tax rate = .18

Price = Tax Basis = $20 per share

$200,000 available. 100,000 shares (investor owns 1,000 shares).

<u>Cash Dividends</u>

Investor receives $2 × 1,000 =	$2,000
Tax (.36)	− 720
	$1,280

<u>Share Repurchase</u>

Investor sells 100 shares	
Investor receives 100 × 20 =	$2,000
(no tax, no taxable gain)	

Stock Price Effect

$t_p = .39$ and $k - g = .01$: t_p could be smaller

$$P_0 = \frac{(1 - t_P)D}{k - g} = \frac{(1 - .39)1.639}{.10 - .09} = \frac{1}{.01} = \$100$$

Div yield equals to 1.639%

Change t_p to zero:

$$P_1 = \frac{1.639}{.10 - .09} = \$164$$

or

$$\frac{P_1}{P_0} = \frac{1}{1 - t_p} = 1.64$$

If price is set by zero tax investors ($k - g = .01$):

$P_0 = P_t = \$164$ No Change

k could change with tax law change.

Stock Price Effect (Initial Price = \$20)

Common Stock Value	\$2,000,000
less (repurchase)	– 200,000
New Value	\$1,800,000

After dividend:

$$P = \frac{1{,}800{,}000}{100{,}000} = \$18$$

After share repurchase (10,000 shares)

$$P = \frac{1{,}800{,}000}{90{,}000} = \$20 \text{ (no Change)}$$

But through time with Div equal to 10% of market capitalization the price will grow at:

$$g = \frac{\text{Div}}{\text{V} - \text{Div}} = \frac{200{,}000}{2{,}000{,}000 - 200{,}000} = 0.111$$

Assumes zero real growth.

$$P_1 = \frac{2{,}000{,}000}{90{,}000} = \$22.22$$

At time 10, the stock price can be expected to be:

$$P_{10} = 20(1.111)^{10} = \$57.30$$

Share Repurchase

1. Stock price effect
2. EPS effect (and other cosmetic changes)
3. Firm buys undervalued stock
4. Partial LBO
5. Tax effects for investor (tax deferral, capital gains tax rate, tax basis protection)
6. Optional dividend for investor (save transaction costs)
7. Firm can buy odd lots of its stock
8. Signal to market (stock is undervalued, etc.)
9. Buy shares for corporate use (avoid dilution)
10. Flexible dividend (for firm and for investors)
11. Best use of cash?

Each of the above deserves expansion.

Some Generalizations

1. The percentage increase in stock price does not depend on (k-g).
2. The magnitude of D (as long as it is positive) does not affect the percentage increase in stock price.
3. The magnitude of t_p is important!

Conclusions

1. For financial strategies to increase value, the firm must have value.
2. Distribution policy is powerful with many facets.
3. With private equity, the recommended strategies tend to be implemented.

Printed in the United States
By Bookmasters